AT YOUR SERVICE

Living the Lessons
of Servant Leadership

Revised Edition (2025)

Charles E. Wheaton Ph.D.

MainSpring Books

Printed in the United States of America

ISBN 979-8-89114-192-6 (sc)
ISBN 979-8-89114-193-3 (e)

Library of Congress Preassigned Control Number: 2025910900

2025.06.17

MainSpring Books
5901 W. Century Blvd
Suite 750
Los Angeles, CA, US, 90045

www.mainspringbooks.com

Dedication

2025

This book is dedicated to all my friends, and colleagues, who have supported me throughout the years and especially my family members who continue to show me through their actions the power of living the lessons of Servant Leadership. In this revised edition, it is dedicated to all of those who I inadvertently left out of the first edition who have struggled to sustain their culture and overcome prejudicial actions, such as, leaders who more accurately represent diversity, equity, and inclusion. These include the contributions of indigenous leaders and leaders of major religious groups.

No one will be able to stand against you all the days of your life. As I was with Moses, I will be with you; I will never leave you nor forsake you. Be strong and courageous, because you will lead these people to inherit the land I swore to their ancestors to give them. "Be strong and very courageous. Be careful to obey all the law my servant Moses gave you; do not turn from it to the right or to the left, that you may be successful wherever you go. Keep this Book of the Law always on your lips; meditate on it day and night, so that you may be careful to do everything written in it. Then you will be prosperous and successful.
Joshua 1:5-8

Table of Contents

Make me a channel of your peace,
Where there is hatred let me bring your love,
Where there is injury your pardon Lord,
And where there's doubt true faith in you.
Lord grant that I may never seek,
So much to be consoled as to console,
To be understood; as to understand,
To be loved as to love with all my soul.
Make me a channel of your peace,
Where there is hatred let me bring your love,
Where there is injury your pardon Lord,
And where there's doubt true faith in you.
Francis of Assisi

Introduction

"Whoever desires to be great among you, let him be your servant. And whoever desires to be first among you, let him be your slave—just as the Son of Man did not come to be served, but to serve, and to give His life a ransom for many."
Matthew 20:26-28

"What kind of world would you want to be born into if you did not know what your social status would be, what your intelligence and natural abilities would be, or what your opportunities in life would be?" These questions posed by Harvard political philosopher, John Rawls, struck me at the core of my being. I believe these are the questions that the practice of "Servant Leadership" attempts to address.

This book, "At Your Service: Living the Lessons of Servant Leadership" will not only include lessons from servant leadership but also from other emerging models of leadership. It will provide a wealth of information and examples describing leadership theory and various styles of leadership that have been identified throughout the literature and those that are currently in use. The lessons will include the importance of understanding the culture of an organization and the use of power. The definition of servant leadership that will be explored has been adapted by Spears from the work of Robert Greenleaf. The key elements of servant leadership, as identified by Spears are listening, empathy, healing, awareness, persuasion, conceptualization, foresight, stewardship, commitment to the growth of others, and building community. Each of these key leadership elements will be described in detail with examples of their application.

This revised edition will attempt to fill in some of the gaps that occurred in the time between the first edition and the present. We have not only undergone a worldwide pandemic, a mass division between political parties in the United States that led to a violent storm on the Capitol Building in Washington, D.C. The United States finally realized that there was no more to gain by continuing to occupy Afghanistan with military troops and support and a new threat has come about has Russian President Putin is determined to take bake the countries that were once a part of Russia. The most prominent in case is the Ukraine, which is served by President Lewinsky, who demonstrates many of the qualities of Servant Leadership. Slowly, the populace is beginning to understand that there is more to gender than the traditional recognition of only male and female choices but there are many who are not traditional male and female and find happiness and love in other choices. Along these same lines, many have accepted that what a woman chooses to do with her body is her choice and belongs to no one else and the choices she makes are very complicated and personal.

Climate change has become a real and consequential issue that must be addressed by all world leaders. Respect and acceptance of all major world religions must be embraced and indigenous peoples throughout the world and primarily in North and South America must be honored and their languages and cultures must be respected and restored. Pope Francis has been chosen to lead and represent the Catholic Church. He is the first Pope to be chosen from South America. He is attempting to alter some of the many barriers that have caused discord within and outside of the Catholic Church. The issues addressed here are in no way inclusive. There are many more.

Identification of effective applications of servant leadership principles in the fields of business, education, religion, and the public sector will be described. It will be demonstrated that these principles apply as much in secular service as they do in the context of religion or spirituality. Finally, suggestions for future effective leadership practices will be referenced. And yes, it is a feel-good kind of read because there is so much in leadership in which to be optimistic. Much of it you have read in other places at other times but if you are anything like me in your passion to increase your leadership potential, you will welcome this compilation of lessons on leadership.

This writing was first inspired by the completion of my doctoral dissertation in 1999 and breathed into flame by encouragement from family and friends and most specifically encouragement from my son, Mark, who has made many trips to Mexico. I have been writing ever since with updates, revisions, and further inspiration. We had made many enjoyable trips to Mexico so I am always eager to go again. I made plans for a trip to Mexico that didn't go as well as the others. I had intended to go to Leon, Guanajuato, Mexico for the purpose of teaching English to adults. I had hoped to become more fluent in Spanish while at the same time providing help to others who wished to learn English. After months of preparation and hopeful anticipation, I found when I arrived in Guanajuato that the folks on the receiving end were not nearly as prepared as I was. Over the years, I have learned that first impressions are critical, and I knew this was not typical of the Mexican culture. On other visits, no matter how poor folks are, I have always experienced fabulous thoughtfulness and attention to my needs.

After an exceedingly brief stay, I was on my way back home feeling very disappointed it didn't work out as I had planned but perhaps, I did not consult God enough on my decision prior to leaving for the trip. Without much delay upon my return, I was asked to help with a new online graduate leadership program at a nearby university. This experience turned out to be a very good one. I was able to learn a lot and was to offer service to other faculty members. I found many staff and faculty members who shared my passion for serving others.

One I especially was fortunate to get to know quite well taught in the teacher education department. She was so knowledgeable about everything and demonstrated the qualities of servant leadership so well. She was an especially good listener and was passionate about meeting the needs of others. On campus and off, she was a champion for social justice. She demonstrated a keen awareness for all cultures, gender differences, and religious practices. She was especially close to our Native American brothers and sisters and immersed herself in their native rituals. Like them, she has great respect for all forms of nature. Unfortunately for us all, she contracted brain cancer and left us five years after she learned of the disease. During those five years, she continued to fill us with as much love and inspiration as she was able.

On subsequent trips to Guanajuato, I learned more about the graciousness of the people, and I did become more adept at using the language. It is a beautiful town with a rich history. I have been able to return numerous times. I am often alone during my time there, but I enjoy my time and the atmosphere.

Recently (1998-2018), according to Eva, N., Robin, M., van Dierendonck, D. and Liden, R., almost 300 articles can be easily accessed. This is exciting, as this growth illustrates that more humane practices of leadership are being studied, modeled, and embraced. We find from Akban (2021), there are representatives from all corners of the globe addressing almost every occupation and profession imaginable. These include anyone from school custodians and first responders to leaders of city, armed forces, and country government positions. In these positions, a variety of issues are promoted. They include, but are not limited to, social justice, disease cures and prevention, educational access, flattening the lines between the rich and the poor, environmental protection, domestic abuse, and business and government corruption.

During this cursory review, it was found that these leaders came from a variety of economic and social backgrounds, cultures, races, gender and spiritual preferences. In a separate contribution by Wolf, W. (2015) in a submission to LinkedIn, we finally see credit given to our "First Persons-Indigenous People." Wolf notes,

> "They know what their source of power is, and they do not abuse that power. Sharing power is one of their best attributes and they are very quick to raise others up who demonstrate their ability to take on leadership roles. They empower everyone around them, and this permeates the entire Tribal government staff. They

are very self-aware, and they have a very high level of compassion for others. They have a gift for knowing when the people need something and if they are in a position to help them, they do so. Servant leadership is part of their DNA. These leaders are always putting others first. Traditionally our leaders would never ask others to do anything that they were not willing to do themselves."

Throughout the text of revised edition of this book, the reader will note scriptural references and examples of servant leadership that have influenced my life since I was very young. These references were not chosen randomly but very specifically to reflect upon while learning or relearning about the leadership issues in the text. One of the many key scriptural verses which describe servant leadership is taken from Matthew 20:26: "Whoever wishes to be great among you most be your servant." This is just one of many verses that come from stories throughout the Bible which show how Jesus Christ demonstrated the effectiveness of service in His leadership. It seems appropriate to me that current and aspiring leaders might also look to this model of service for guidance in practicing effective leadership.

I have no doubt that most other religions have as many inspirational lessons from their spiritual leaders that have been passed down through the ages. The Christian faith does not have a monopoly on leadership lessons. Each faith tradition has been blessed with books of wisdom and inspiration, whether they be Jew, Muslim, Bahai, Hindu, Mormon, or Buddhist. In some of my previous reading, it has been pointed out that twenty-three different faith traditions have similar messages for the "Golden Rule." (Do unto others as you would have them do unto you.) Love of God, creation, and each other is at the heart of each of these faith traditions' beliefs. It is about humility, justice, and mercy that promotes freedom, equality, equity, and dignity for all people. Even the Dalai Lama has been quoted to say in a bit of levity, "If you think you are too small to make a difference, try sleeping with a mosquito."

In the verse quoted above from the gospel of Matthew, we see how Jesus demonstrated the effectiveness of service in leadership. In another account, Jesus demonstrated servant leadership to His co-workers by washing their feet (John 13:1-17). Jesus also showed us by the followers that He chose how He would patiently call out the best in each of them. The followers he chose were not much different than you or me but Jesus sought ordinary people with a wide range of strengths and abilities to show how each of us possesses valuable leadership skills.

In like manner, Paul and other leaders who aspire to lead, teach that leadership is to live, to love, to learn, and to leave a legacy. It is turning one person's talent into extraordinary performance. It is capitalizing on each person's talent(s). In the letter to Philemon, Paul used commitment, dedication, service, wisdom, and passion to move followers-Onesimus and Philemon-from dependence to independence or, better yet, interdependence. Paul was equipping his followers by day-to-day coaching, showing them the vision, and preparing them for the final exam from the very first day. He helped them by guiding them to discover and develop their own individual strengths.

As the followers discovered and developed their own strengths, the leader moved them toward team leadership. He instilled in them courage, honesty, and integrity which developed a trusting relationship. Trust is developed by a firm reliance on the mutual integrity, ability and character of the leader and followers. Paul modeled this integrity by being who he was no matter where he was or who he was with. Paul developed team leadership by accentuating the positive in each person, realizing potential and specifically recognizing and praising progress.

This leadership progression has the ability to cause personal and social change, such as the acceptance and forgiveness of Onesimus as a Christian brother and ultimately the social change regarding slavery. Paul reinforces his leadership act by reinforcing the actions with measures of accountability and praise. He tells Philemon, "Prepare a room for me. I'll be coming soon."

Emphasizing this same need for leaving a legacy and creating a positive impact on others, Gloria Burgess (2008), in her book, "Dare to wear your soul on the outside" writes:

Like the currents of a mighty river, your legacy is always in motion, continuously flowing. Your legacy is your magnum opus, your supreme and magnificent life's work. Your life is something of a relay race, and what you pass on is the precious baton of your values and beliefs, your principles and practices, your decisions and choices, the sum total of who you are.

Quoting from another source on moral living, Haines and Yaggy, in 1882 shared in their book "The Royal Path of Life," how each of us makes a significant difference, whether we intend it or not. They stated:

Every man is a missionary, now and forever, for good or for evil, whether he intends it or not. He may be a blot, radiating his dark influence outward to the very circumference of society, or he may be a blessing, spreading benedictions over the length and breadth of the world; but a blank he cannot be. The seeds that are sown in life spring up in harvests of blessings or in harvests of sorrow. Whether our influence is great or small, whether it is for good or evil, it lasts; it lives somewhere, within some limit, and is operative wherever it is. We live and we die; but the good or evil we do lives after us, and is not "buried with our bones.

One kernel is felt in a hogshead—one drop of water helps to swell the ocean—a spark of fire helps to give light to the world. You are a small man, passing amid the crowd you are hardly noticed; but you have a drop, a spark within you that may be felt for eternity. None are too small—too feeble—too poor to be of service.

It is really for this reason that I write this book. I have been blessed with many in my life that have modeled these lessons of servant leadership and I too hope that in some small way I might do the same.

My father modeled all of the characteristics I didn't want to incorporate in my own life and even this I guess I can count as a blessing or at least a lesson to try and live a different kind of life than he did. I have to admit, I am not always successful in all regards, but I remain determined to live a life that exemplifies service to others. Since we moved so frequently, people will ask, "what did your father do?" I have to reply that I don't remember that he ever had a steady job. He was drunk most of the time that he was awake and much of the time he was physically and mentally abusive to our Mom. I believe his own experiences growing up in foster homes and serving in hostile areas during his time in the military left him unable to cope with life.

Like many women of her era, Mom put up with Dad's drunkenness and abuse for a long time and never gave up hope, consequently we moved 23 times from rental to rental throughout the Seattle/Puget Sound area of Washington State before I reached the age of 18. We lived in most of the subsidized rent projects for short periods of time and enrolled in ten different schools prior to my graduation. I'm not sure how Mom pulled it off, but of course it was many years ago, but it never seemed to be an option for us to attend any school except a Catholic School. There always seemed to be room for us and the parish was always very welcoming to us although I am confident we didn't contribute a dime toward tuition as there was no dime to contribute. I have a feeling the St. Vincent de Paul Society took pretty good care of us but I don't really have any way of knowing for sure.

Although, not having what most would consider the advantages of coming from a privileged background, I had those few special people in my life that believed in me and pushed me even when I rebelled.

At the age of 15, I had the opportunity to work at one of the finest restaurants in Seattle, Washington. I learned from some of the best food service professionals in the industry how effective and enjoyable it is to provide service to others. I continued my close connections with these professionals throughout the years and have learned that successful leaders in any field are adept at arranging their smorgasbord of services into a feast that feeds the needs and values of those they serve.

At the age of 23, I experienced the same kind of commitment to service when I accepted my first teaching position. The principal I worked with continually modeled service to others and a strong commitment to moral leadership. Later on in my career, while serving as an elementary principal myself, this same leader modeled servant leadership to me at a higher level while he was director of elementary programs. Working in impoverished communities throughout much of my career and being a part of mission trips and visits to the poor in Mexico, I have been able to witness countless acts of servant leadership.

More than thirty years later, experiences such as these continue to compel me to study and to attempt to apply the many exciting elements of effective leadership.

This is what it is all about for me. A.G. Lafley, CEO of Proctor and Gamble stated it so well:

> I want to know everything I can about leadership. Because I don't think leaders are born. I don't believe you spring fully armored out of the head of Athena to slay Hector in battle. I believe leaders choose to lead at some point in their life. And it's because they have a call to action. They have a calling. They have something they want to make happen. They choose to be part of a change that they want to see in the world going around them, and they choose to step forward, and they choose to take the risk of leadership…the key is to be yourself. Be who you are. Be passionate about who you are and what you care about, and have fun (Tichy & Bennis, p. 238).

With all the effort I believe each of one of us puts forth to attempt to be better leaders and to try and convince ourselves and others that there is no prejudice in our lives, I believe we all carry around petty thoughts that place us above others. With these thoughts of prejudice comes more division between us than unity among us.

Throughout our world right now, it seems we are fueled with so many instances of hate toward each other. The article entitled, "Who, Me? Racist?" by Whitney Parnell spoke to this topic. At first blush I suspected this was from a white male's point of view, but I submit it could be any of us. It certainly is me and I hate to admit it. (https://sojo.net/biography/whitney-parnell) I am the guy who the author says is philosophically against racism so it couldn't be me. I stopped to think about all the other areas where I am philosophically opposed to discrimination. But set me alone in the middle of a group of people that don't look, believe or think like me, how comfortable am I? Do I even experience a degree of fear and anxiety? You bet I do, and I am philosophically against all the reasons we find to hate each other. For me, I'm ashamed to admit, it includes not only race but sex, nationality, religion; even within my own so-called Christian faith where we find every miniscule reason not to accept each other as Jesus did. My acceptance of others also depends on social and economic status, appearance, habits, addictions, abilities and where people live or don't live. We must love ourselves before we are able to love others, but God has a lot of work to do on me and He is running out of time.

What would the world be like if we could all live by the following words from Matthew?

> In Matthew 25: 35-40 He says: "For I was hungry, and you gave me something to eat, I was thirsty and you gave me something to drink, I was a stranger and you invited me in, 36 I needed clothes and you clothed me, I was sick and you looked after me, I was in prison and you came to visit me. 'Then the righteous will answer him, 'Lord, when did we see you hungry and feed you, or thirsty and give you something to drink? When did we see you a stranger and invite you in, or needing clothes and clothe you? When did we see you sick or in prison and go to visit you?' "The King will reply, 'Truly

I tell you, whatever you did for one of the least of these brothers and sisters of mine, you did for me.'

Similar words of hope were written on a Christmas card I received from a dear friend: "Imagine a world where people live in harmony, where love comes in all colors, where giving comes from the heart, where peace lights the earth…"

"He has shown you people what is good; and what
does the Lord require of you but to do justly, to love
mercy, and to walk humbly with your god?
Micah 6:8

What do the Gurus say about Leadership?

So, what do the gurus have to say about leadership? Peter Drucker says:

> "Leadership is the lifting of a man's vision to higher sights, the raising of a person's performance to a higher standard, the building of a person's personality beyond its normal limitations. Nothing better prepares the ground for such leadership than a spirit of management that confirms in the day-to-day practices of the organization the strict principles of conduct and responsibility, high standards of performance, and respect for the individuals and their work." Drucker-Managing the Non-Profit Organization 1992

At Microsoft Corporation (2006), they state: "Great leaders define, shape, and inspire the human experience. In a world of ideas, we are adrift without the leaders who realize them. For this reason, effective leadership is critical to the success of any organization." Microsoft has identified competencies for building successful leaders in education. These include but are not limited to individual excellence, courage, operational skills, organizational skills, strategic skills, and results. Each of these broad categories is broken down into smaller skills and it is possible for an individual to do an assessment of strengths and areas in which to work to improve as an educational leader.

Leadership is an issue that affects all of us. In some way or other, each of us has a leadership role to play. Leadership must be a selfless act that considers the needs of others first. Consideration is given to what is right for the greater good rather than one's own interests.

In a very recent search (October 2013) of Academic Search Premier, 47,000 articles dealing with leadership were identified. This will be outdated before I finish revising this book. What follows are just a smattering of those definitions and descriptions of leadership that come from some of the leading researchers on the subject of leadership.

Although not the earliest research in leadership, one of the classical theories of leadership was McGregor's (1960) categories of Theory X and Theory Y. Theory X assumed the average person to be lazy, dislike responsibility, prefer to be led, is inherently self-centered, is indifferent to organizational needs, and is resistant to change. Therefore, it was believed people in a Theory X workforce must be forced or bribed to perform. They are motivated by money or anxiety about their security and they lack creativity. Leaders who accept Theory X assumptions attempt to structure, control, and closely supervise their subordinates.

Theory Y, on the other hand, assumes people basically have a desire to do the right thing, can be self-directed, and will accept the overall mission and objectives of the organization. Theory Y assumes people want to work and will strive to reach their potential. Creativity and ingenuity are valued and widely encouraged among all workers. Leaders who accept Theory Y assumptions are concerned bout their coworker's needs. Under Theory Y, there is a strong relationship between the leader and the followers and they are interdependent upon each other.

Having had the opportunity to work closely with McGregor, Bennis (Heil, et. al. 2000) remembered that McGregor stressed the fundamental importance of dealing with the human side of enterprise. He believed managers had to see their employees not as cogs in the machine, but as living beings with individual goals. This was not, in his view, a limitation, but a condition that opened up countless opportunities. When organized properly, groups of people working together could realize their aspirations in a far more powerful and deep-rooted manner than they could have imagined. Those leaders who saw these opportunities and made the bold organizational choice to realize their potential, both individually and collectively, would leapfrog anyone with a more traditional mindset.

Rost (1991) found in his research that the word leadership is relatively new. In 1818, Webster first defined leadership as merely "the state or condition of a leader." This certainly doesn't tell us much in terms of the way we refer to leadership now. The definition has evolved over time and has taken on many more complex elements of human dynamics.

According to Rost (1991), in the 1950's and 1960's, leadership scholars defined the term as a behavioral relationship that influenced people toward developing shared goals. The 1970's literature showed a shift from the group approach of the social psychologist to the organizational behavior approach of the management scholars. Leadership for the 1980's was dominated by the message that leadership is basically doing what the leader wants done. It followed the view of leadership referred to as the great man/woman theory. Three leaders of the 1980's that followed this model were political leaders Gorbachev, Reagan, and Thatcher. Leaders of this type have been placed in remarkable circumstances that have permitted their leadership skills to be manifested.

In addressing relationships necessary for effective leadership, Rost identified four essential elements that all must be precisely identifiable if any relationship is to be defined as leadership: (a) the relationship must be based on influence; (b) leaders and followers are the people in the relationship; (c) the leaders must intend real changes; and (d) they must develop mutual purposes (p. 104).

Block believed leadership is really motivated by passion, spirit, integrity, and comes from the heart. If we are to agree, then Rost's requirement for a precise definition is not reasonable. To help explain that he had not overlooked the qualities of the heart, Rost suggested that the ethics and morality of leadership have to do with the process of leadership, rather than the content. Much more inclined to go along with Block, Depree (1989) had devoted an entire book to describing leadership as an art and concluded, "Leadership is much more an art, a belief, and a condition of the heart, rather than a set of things to do" (p. 148).

In like manner, Souba (2011) described the four ontological pillars of leadership. They are awareness, commitment, integrity, and authenticity. Ontology relates to the nature of being a leader as opposed to the doing and performing of leadership tasks. Ontology answers the question: How does the person live and experience his leadership? The awareness piece of the equation is the ability to perceive, feel, or to be conscious of events, objects, or sensations. This is a very important part of leadership and precedes the doing part of leadership. Most of those who are referenced below share these basic tenets or pillars as Souba refers to them.

As noted above, effective contemporary leadership theories share at their roots several characteristics. These include putting others first; expressing in totality that which is professed in words, taking time for introspection and meditation; and being committed to ideals and to the group. Gardner (1990) reminds us if we look at the array of societies described by historians and anthropologists; we cannot find an instance of a healthy society in which humans have not devised a framework of values, norms of conduct, and a moral order. These are the characteristics espoused by Greenleaf and others as those of a servant leader.

Hodgkinson (1991) noted the need for leadership where management skills are combined with ethics and values. With the transition toward more employee participation in decision-making, those who aspire to leadership need to replace control with other models of leadership. The leadership style that has been traditionally practiced has been an autocratic, top-down style of leadership. This style of leadership relied upon rigid hierarchical structure, competition, and control to bring about results. Although this model is changing, many still subscribe to it.

I see the exception to this participatory model failing when, for example, a union dominated workforce competes and undermines the efforts to promote inclusionary practices. A system such as this creates discord rather than harmony. There become constant power struggles where the attempt at participation turns into bargaining.

This effort toward developing a more participatory model may fail when an opposing group of workers competes with and dominates or even undermines the leadership's attempt to promote inclusionary practices. A system such as this creates discord rather than harmony. There become constant power struggles where what was intended as collegial efforts toward participation turns into antagonistic bargaining.

According to Senge (1990), effective leaders need to focus on the shared vision. He notes one of the deepest desires underlying shared vision is the desire to be connected to a larger purpose and to one another. The spirit of connection is fragile and it is undermined whenever we lose our respect for one another and for each other's views. So the commitments we make as leaders are not just to ourselves, but to all those with whom we share the vision. Senge shares one of my favorite descriptions of outstanding leadership. He states:

> Most of the outstanding leaders I have worked with are neither tall nor especially handsome; they are often mediocre public speakers; they do not stand out in a crowd; and they do not mesmerize an attending audience with their brilliance or eloquence. Rather, what distinguishes them is the clarity and persuasiveness of their ideas, the depth of their commitment, and their openness to continually learning more. They do not "have the answer."
> But they do instill confidence in those around them that, together, "we can learn whatever we need to learn in order to achieve the results we truly desire."

As for me, I am short of stature with an extra ounce or more of fat and getting more physically weathered by the day and I often get so excited speaking that I break into a bit of a stutter. But I have a passion that compels me to continue to learn about working and serving those in greatest need.

Collins (2001) and his "Good to Great" team established that the specific type of leadership did make a difference. Leaders of the good-to-great companies were not high profile and celebrity focused. Rather they demonstrated a personal humility and professional will revealing a fierce resolve to do what was best for the company, not the leader him or herself.

Holifield (1993) echoed a similar sentiment. He indicated a leader needs to commit to something outside of oneself. He needs to be part of creating something he cares about so he can endure the sacrifice, risk, and adventure that commitment entails. He also noted, Philosopher Immanuel Kant emphasized this same kind of conscience in his categorical imperative: to act in such a way that one always treats others with respect and that we act out of duty regardless of the reward. In dysfunctional organizations, a leader is challenged when she often finds that the common good or the act of duty is being replaced with a demand for an additional monetary stipend for every act performed.

Bennis (1989) described the basic ingredients of leadership as integrity, dedication, magnanimity, humility, openness, and creativity. Burns (1978) defined leadership as leaders inducing followers to act for certain goals that represent the values and the motivations—the wants and needs, the aspirations and expectations—of both leaders and followers. The genius lies in the manner in which the leaders see and act on their own and their followers' values and motivations.

Bass (1990) summarized a wide variety of definitions of effective leadership as the interaction among members of a group that initiates and maintains improved expectations, and the competence of the group to solve problems or to attain goals.

He stated:

> Interpersonal competence is fundamental to successful and effective leadership. What may be involved is the ability to communicate, the willingness and ability to promote individual relationships with others, authenticity, caring, and the ability to handle conflict,

and especially the qualities of insight and empathy. Particular attention has been paid to the extent to which leadership requires insight and empathy.

As will be noted later in the discussion of Servant Leadership, the qualities of insight and empathy were important elements embraced by Robert Greenleaf. Throughout the literature, we continue to see it is the consciousness of values, a focus on others, and moral decision-making that must be present in effective leadership. A long time ago, Paul wrote to Timothy reminding him that an overseer (leader) must be above reproach, with one spouse, who is temperate, prudent, respectable, hospitable, able to teach, not addicted to wine or pugnacious, but gentle, peaceable, and free from the love of money (1 Timothy 3:2-4).

Leadership consultant Batten (1997) wrote: "Leaders who are simply getters are yesterday! Leaders, who learn from, teach, serve, and empower others—particularly their customers, clients, and others— are tomorrow. He also emphasized that leaders must expand and empower, not compress, repress, suppress, or depress. They must build on strengths, not focus on weaknesses. Transactional leaders of the past led by making promises, offering rewards, or attempting to correct weaknesses, by threatening with disciplinary actions of punishments. If strengths are reinforced and moral character traits are recognized, it is often not necessary to reward or threaten, and the identified areas of weakness will improve with a more positive approach to leadership.

More than twenty years ago, Sociologist Ray (1997) found in a study of 50 million "cultural creatives" that Americans are becoming more concerned with caring relationships and personal development and are more open to creating a positive future. This emerging group values altruism, authenticity, optimism, and social consciousness. I believe these qualities still hold true today.

Therefore, as leaders, we must value those with whom we work enough to cultivate what many have referred to as the ABC's. Fawcett, et al. (2008) described the ABC's in a study of characteristics that were found to promote an inspiring workplace. These important characteristics which have been found to capture the heart of workers and unleash their energy and insight are affirmation, belonging, and competence.

The authors in this study state: "Affirmation involves positive reinforcement that tells workers they make a difference and are valued."

Cultivating the ABC's of an Inspiring Workplace
Fawcett, Brau, Rhoads, & Whitlark

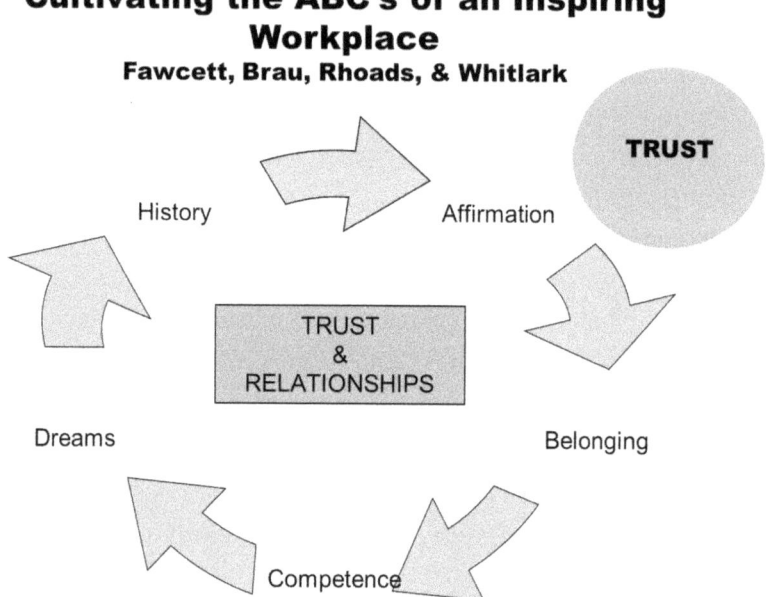

Belonging is the second characteristic, and two aspects of belonging were identified. First was personal belonging where workers felt that through their work, personal and family financial security needs were being met. Secondly was the belonging which makes the worker feel connected socially to other workers and the organization. Competence is the third characteristic and refers to the leader's ability to recognize and encourage an individual's unique strengths and capabilities. When an organization and its leadership recognize the value in cultivating the basic needs of affirmation, belonging, and competence a successful workplace culture is developed which promotes creativity, learning, and the desire for helping others to succeed. The authors referenced a comment by a Fortune 500 senior executive who stated: "People are either the bridge or the barrier." Recognition of these important ABC's provides more assurance that people will be the bridge. It is these ABC's that fill our basic hunger that may be as important to our overall health as food and drink. I submit unless these ABC's are present, it is very difficult to imagine a "D" which is a dream which in turn will bring about "E" which is effectiveness. My additions of "D" and "E" may sound a bit "corny" but it provides a pneumonic device that brings it all together for me. A colleague added another twist to this as he offered that in order for any of the ABC's to occur there must be an attempt between people to learn of each other's history or culture so that authentic gestures of affirmation, belonging, and competence are bestowed on another. As a result of all of this, trust is developed.

All of this really began as the example of servant leadership found so often in the Bible. Just as God created our bodies so that our many parts complement each other and compensate for each other when one part is missing or wounded, He has also created the communal body of Christ to complement and compensate so we can use our special gifts to serve each other.

In Corinthians 12, we are told: "For even as the body is one and yet has many members, and all the members of the body, though they are many, are one body, so also is Christ. For by one Spirit we were all baptized into one body, whether Jews or Greeks, whether slaves or free, and we were all made to drink of one Spirit." And a little bit earlier in the same chapter, Paul explains that there are varieties of gifts, of ministries, and of effects, but the same God who works all things in all persons. One is given the word of wisdom, another knowledge; to another faith, to another gifts of healing, miracles, or prophecy, and to another the distinguishing of spirits, or various kinds of tongues or the interpretation of tongues. But one and the same Spirit does all these things, distributing to each one individually just as He wills.

We need "with." By using our own individual talents and skills to lift up others, we are able to help transform a crowd into a community, a community united in their need for one another. I am reminded of the picture of the turtle on top of the fencepost with the caption: "When you see a turtle on a fencepost, you know he didn't get there by himself." None of us can claim success without a lot of support from others.

Christ empowers each one of us to perform our own miracles of creating community when we remove barriers to include outsiders, where we welcome the rejected and forgotten to our tables, where we give of what little we have, joyfully and gratefully, for the sake of others, where we welcome one another as we would welcome Jesus.

Jesus makes do with what is at hand. He breaks us open so that we have the capacity to be, and to do far more than we otherwise could have imagined. Through His power we can become the kind of leaders that are needed in our family, our community, and our workplace. John Dunne put it this way, "No man is an Island, entire of itself; every one is a piece of the continent, a part of the main."

Archbishop Desmond Tutu (2000) of South Africa provides an entertaining parable which he shared at the Brandeis University Commencement. It went like this: "A traveler happened by and said, "That's not a chicken; that's an eagle." The farmer said, "No, it's just a funny-looking chicken." The farmer gave the bird to the traveler, who took it up to a mountain peak and said, "Fly, eagle, fly." And the eagle soared away. Of course, the lesson is that if you believe in people they will surpass your expectations.

Jaworski (1996) said, "Leadership is all about the release of human possibilities." One of the central requirements is the capacity to inspire the followers to help them become focused and operate at the peak of their performance ability. It is imperative that leaders acknowledge the belief that people matter and their input is valued.

Wheatley (1994) recognized that more frequently than in the past, leadership is being described within its relationship to followership, empowerment, and leader accessibility. Moral and ethical questions are also considered key elements in relationships between leaders and staff.

A public opinion poll conducted in 2001 asked participants to rate professions according to how they see them carrying the highest standards of honesty and ethics. The top five professions, according to the results of this survey were nurses, pharmacists, veterinarians, medical doctors, and elementary and secondary teachers. It isn't surprising when we think about these professions; we note that they all have one thing in common. People in each of these professions serve others in a more personal way than most other vocations. The perceptions people have regarding our honesty and ethical behavior in the workplace are strongly influenced by how caring they believe we are in our professions.

Yukl (2002) points out a variety of these leadership functions which include the following:

- Leaders help interpret the meaning of events.
- Leaders build agreement around objectives and strategies.
- Leaders build task commitment and optimism.
- Leaders develop mutual trust and cooperation.
- Leaders strengthen collective identity.
- Leaders coordinate and organize activities.
- Leaders encourage and facilitate collective learning.
- Leaders obtain necessary resources and support.
- Leaders develop and empower people.
- Leaders promote social justice and morality.

Shwahn and Spady, (2002) say, "Present day leaders must be more like Jesus than John Wayne, more like Gandhi than Vince Lombardi and more like Mother Teresa than Machiavelli."

Recall Niccolo Machiavelli (1910)who was a political philosopher and diplomat during the Renaissance, and who is most famous for his political treatise, "The Prince." For Machiavelli, there was no moral basis on which to judge the difference between legitimate and illegitimate uses of power. Rather, he was a power-hungry autocrat who ruled by the notion that the ends justify the means whether those means be noble or not.

Kouzes and Posner (1995) believe we are presently in a leadership crisis. They point out some absolute maxims regarding effective leadership. Emotions are a key factor in the way strong leaders discuss their leadership. Their passion for their organization is clear. Strong leaders are close to those they serve and often refer to their colleagues as an organizational family. Followers remember what leaders do, and their actions within the daily operations will often determine whether or not they are followed over time. Leadership is a process rather than a place.

Professor of Leadership at Fuller Theological Seminary, Dr. J. Robert Clinton (1993) describes five New Testament Biblical models of leadership. They are referred to as the stewardship model, the servant model, the intercessor model, the shepherd model, and the harvest model. The stewardship model suggests an accountability to God; the servant model uses leadership capacities to serve followers, the intercessor model is founded on prayer for a particular ministry, shepherd leaders empathize with followers seeking to assess where they are and to help meet their needs and develop them toward their kingdom potential, and harvest leaders have a leadership style that is fundamentally task oriented. I would suggest that the models that most closely resemble those embraced in this book are the servant and shepherd models.

As a person studies leadership, it is also appropriate to consider brain research and multiple intelligences. It has been alleged that management is more of a left-brain activity and leadership is more inclined to use of the right brain. Devising systems of rules and organization and applying them systematically are left-brain activities whereas thinking outside of the box in more creative ways is a right-brain leadership activity. There have also been discussions and research around the nature of intelligence. There are theories about multiple intelligence, emotional intelligence, and spiritual intelligence. Howard Gardner (1999) is most often credited with the study of multiple intelligences while Daniel Goleman (2006) is credited with the study of emotional intelligence which includes a range of abilities, including self-awareness, self-control, and empathy. Spiritual intelligence involves the ability to see the connections between diverse things and to be inspired by vision and values. Paul showed in many of his writings how we are all connected and interrelated.

Co-workers or team members need meaningful involvement in the processes, the projects, and the purposes that affects them. Coach "K" (2000) of Duke University relates: "At our first meeting, I give the team only one rule to live by." The rule he speaks of is very general. It is simply: "Don't do anything detrimental to yourself." He says he doesn't have to tell the players all the details because the upperclassmen will do that. This, in turn, fosters additional leadership and leadership on any team should be plural, not singular. Coach "K" believes, too many rules get in the way of leadership. They just put you in a box and, sooner or later, a rule-happy leader will wind up in a situation where he wants to use some discretion but is forced to go along with some decree that he himself has concocted. This year as Coach K has announced his retirement, he has left his legacy on innumerable athletes, their families and the community.

Robinson (2002) described the traits of a secure leader and how they need to be other-centered. He stated:

> Leading is not about me. My duty is to see that this organization executes its mission with excellence and strength. Any needs I have to be a star or marionette of that execution steals from this organization and misdirects my energy. At the point I let go of focusing on me, my role changes. I become the dispatcher rather

than the driver, the coach rather than the player, the resource rather than the watchdog, and the interpreter rather than the expert (p. 52).

William Law, an Anglican priest in Northamptonshire, England in the 1700's gave these instructions about letting go of oneself and putting one's focus on others in his devotional classic, "A Serious Call to a devout and holy life." He said:

Let every day be a day of humility:

- ❖ condescend to all the weaknesses and infirmities of your fellow creatures,
- ❖ cover their fragilities,
- ❖ love their excellencies,
- ❖ encourage their virtues,
- ❖ relieve their wants,
- ❖ rejoice in their prosperities,
- ❖ show compassion at their distress,
- ❖ receive their friendship,
- ❖ overlook their unkindness,
- ❖ forgive their malice,
- ❖ be a servant of servants, and
- ❖ condescend to the lowliest offices of the lowest of mankind.

These are great lessons for any leader at any place or time. It's about who you want to become. Jeff Immelt of GE told a class of MBA's: "The first part of leadership is an intense journey into yourself; it's a commitment and an intense journey into your soul" (Tichy & Bennis, (2000) p. 241).

In a poem by Oriah Mountain Dreamer (1994) entitled "The Invitation, Oriah shares similar thoughts as Immelt:

It doesn't interest me who you know, or how you came to be here. I want to know if you will stand in the center of the fire with me and not shrink back.

It doesn't interest me where or what or with whom you have studied. I want to know what sustains you from the inside when all else falls away.

I want to know if you can be alone with yourself and if you truly like the company you keep in the empty moments.

To a great extent, we are who we are and each of us has to do the best we can with what we have been given. There are a variety of personality assessments that can help us determine how effective we might be in a leadership position. One of the most common studies of leader traits is commonly referred to as the Big Five model. It identified five major personality traits. These traits are neuroticism or emotional stability, extroversion, openness to experience, agreeableness, and conscientiousness. There continue to be many studies which attempt to identify which of the Big Five plays the greatest part in leadership effectiveness.

Who's in charge around here anyway?

Power and Influence

Power or influence is a given condition in the role of leadership. But with power comes responsibility. Our nation was founded on this principle. The symbols on our one-dollar bill are a constant reminder of this. On the back of the dollar bill on the left-hand side, you see the back of the Great Seal of the United States which is the three-sided image of a pyramid. Each of the points of the pyramid has a special significance in terms of responsibility. The two points at the base represent political and economic responsibility and the highest point of the pyramid represents social and religious responsibility. Hovering over this pyramid is an eye, which is the eye of the Almighty smiling down upon us as we strive to live up to our responsibilities.

In her book, "Peace and Power," Peggy Chinn (2013) contrasts how power can either be used to impose one's will or it can be used to bring about peace. A few examples of power over include the power of results, division, force, hierarchy and command. These are contrasted with the power of process, wholeness, collectivity, solidarity, and sharing.

Power is something that is granted or assumed by an individual who attempts to affect change. Sometimes power is interpreted negatively, but it need not be. Power has been defined as one person's degree of influence over others to the extent that conformity of obedience follows.

Pelicer and Anderson (1995, pp. 35-36), built upon the work of French and Raven from 1960, and identified five different types of power.

The sources of power French and Raven identified were: reward power, coercive power, legitimate power, expert power, and referent power. These sources of power come from either formal or personal bases. Formal power is based on an individual's position in an organization. Personal power comes from an individual's unique characteristics. Reward power comes from the hope that one might receive rewards such as pay raises, bonuses, recognition, and/or promotions. Coercive power is based on fear of the negative results that might occur if one fails to comply. Each of these is dependent upon being able to give something or take something away. Legitimate power is based on one's authoritative position in the organization. Expert power is influence wielded as a result of expertise, special skill, or knowledge. Referent power is based on association with a person who has desirable resources or traits. Referent power is manifested out of admiration of another and a desire to be like that person. Of course, few leaders operate exclusively using one type of power or influence as they need to consider all dynamics as noted in the following.

Hoy and Miskel (2010) offer some compelling ideas regarding the use of power. They point out the power games and political tactics that people often use in their struggles to influence others. I say people but truly, we all use these games and tactics to our advantage at times. In the area of political games, organizational members have three choices in playing power games. They can either leave the organization, 2) stay and be a player and have their voice be heard, or 3) they can stay and be a loyal to the organization. Hoy and Miskel also identify a number of tactics that are used for a variety of purposes in communication and thereby influencing decision-making.

These include:

1. Ingratiating which is gaining favors by doing favors
2. Networking with influential persons which is gaining influence by courting

3. Managing Information by manipulating information to one's advantage
4. Managing impressions which creates a positive imagine by appearance
5. Coalition building which bands together with others to achieve goals
6. Scapegoating which shifts the blame to others for bad outcomes
7. Increasing indispensability by making yourself indispensable
8. Spinning the truth which puts the best face on the facts
9. Flattering which is artificial praise of others, and finally;
10. Gassing which is getting attention of others and thereby, standing out.

These different uses and abuses of power must be considered as we observe our politicians at work. Politicians buy their positions at the expense of wealthy donors while citing one of the greatest current crises as financial recessions. However, we continue to finance the most expensive and mean-spirited political campaigns in the history of our country. I thought we were in the worst economic times in our history but apparently this does not apply to politicians and those who fund them.

How can we say we are unable to afford health care and education when millions of dollars are spent on campaigns and warfare while at the same time, people are homeless and starving and cannot afford to take care of basic health care needs? What if these same politicians had to submit to a test of servant leadership traits? Would they stand up to the test? Do those served grow as persons; do they, while being served, become healthier, wiser, freer, more autonomous, and more likely themselves to become servants?

Dr. William F. Kumuyi (2007, December) in his description of "the functions of a servant-leader" tells us, "The objective is to enhance the growth of individuals in the organization and increase teamwork and personal involvement. The Mayor of Newark, New Jersey, Cory Booker, at least made an attempt to understand the plight of the poor by living on the amount of money that is allotted to the poor as food coupons. Sure, he did take this on as a way of life but at least made a greater attempt than most politicians who only talk about how they understand.

Throughout all of this our phones continue to ring off the hook as, candidates from all of the parties request millions of dollars so they can spend it on demeaning ads that are designed to show that they are more righteous than their opponent. There's something wrong with this picture. How can one be so righteous while at the same time be slinging mud? Someone missed the part from Ephesians that says, "Let no evil talk come out of your mouths, but only what is useful for building up, as there is need to, so that your words may give grace to those who hear." Woe! I don't hear any adherence to those words in the campaign ads. So, why not try putting some of the advice from those who have studied leadership into positive action?

San Juan (2005) discussed the integration of inner and outer power dynamics and the challenge of reflection, integration, and servant-leadership. He believes leaders must have both of these power perspectives: power without or exteriority, and power within or interiority. The sense of exteriority challenges the leader to know and comprehend the power dynamics of his or her environment and setting. On the other hand, the sense of interiority challenges the leader to grasp and grapple with power within the self through psychological, philosophical, and spiritual frames of understanding. The effective leader needs to exercise both exteriority and interiority. Not to have one or the other leads to a limited view of power and reality that is bifurcated and disjointed. A leader is called to attend to both internal and external realities, to both self and environment.

Tom Sanders (2002), Yahoo Senior Executive, noted: "The most powerful force in business isn't greed, fear, or even the raw energy of unbridled competition. The most powerful force in business is love." By love he means the selfless promotion of the growth of others. Love is the killer App. Every member of the team depends on each and every other member to contribute. It is about sharing the intangibles of the business with all team members. These intangibles are the organization's knowledge, network, and compassion. These are the values that give meaning to a career and an effective organization.

I am encouraged by the sensitive words of compassion by Former President Dwight D. Eisenhower (1947) as he spoke about the role of power and its influence on humankind during times of war. He stated:

> Every gun that is made, every warship launched, every rocket fired signifies, in the final sense, a theft from those who hunger and are not fed, those who are cold and are not clothed. This world in arms is not spending money alone. It is spending the sweat of its laborers, the genius of its scientists, and the hopes of its children.

Many years and many wars later, we have still not learned from Eisenhower's message. The abuse of power lives on while many die as a result. In 2012, the number of soldiers who committed suicide outnumbered the number of soldiers killed in combat. We have even developed a definition to justify war. We aptly call it "just war." I have a problem with this. When you go about searching to find and kill, how is it possible to call it a just war or ethical conduct or an act of charity? It is like our parents use to say, "I know this hurts but I'm doing it for your own good. Someday, you will thank me." However, in the case of war and killing, there isn't a someday in the future.

The role of power and influence are about the hope and good future which comes from these words of Jeremiah. It is not about hurting others.

> "I say this because I know what I am planning for you. I have good plans for you, not plans to hurt you. I will give you hope and a good future."
> Jeremiah 29:1

What causes us to do what we do?

Culture

Earlier in this book, I referenced Peggy Chinn (2013) from her book, "Peace and Power." In the opening of one of her chapters, she quotes these fabulous statements from Margo Adair regarding a "Community for the Future." She states:

> "Imagine how it feels to always belong—belong in a diversified community, for it is the diversity in nature that gives the web of life its strength and cohesion. Imagine a time where everyone welcomes diversity in people because they know that is wheat gives community its richness, its strength, its cohesion."

With this dream, it is possible that company cultures could take on a spirit that ranges from limiting to inspiring. Fawcett et al (2008) quote John Epps, founding member of IAF (International Association of Facilitators) as he states:

> When spirit is present, doing business with the organization is a delight, when it's missing; working with the company is a drag, whether as a customer, a vendor, or a staff member. Spirit may be intangible, but its effects permeate the entire system and determine

the quality of output. It's too important to be left to happenstance.

Organizations of all kinds are made up of people of all kinds. As San Juan emphasized the need to attend to both internal and external realities, we see that this is directly related to the need for leaders to consider the culture of their organization. Palmer (2000) expressed this challenge very clearly: "A leader is someone with the power to project either shadow or light into some part of the world and onto the lives of the people who dwell there." He goes on to say: "A leader shapes the ethos (culture) in which others must live, an ethos (culture) as light filled as heaven or as shadowy as hell." Leaders communicate values and expectations by their actions. How a leader demonstrates loyalty, self-sacrifice, and service beyond the call of duty creates a very strong message of what the leader feels is important and necessary.

Leadership resources are loaded with references to what culture is and how it is played out. The culture within an organization is revealed by the way things are done. It is the manifestation of shared values, beliefs, behaviors, heroes, and system of written and unwritten policies, practices, and procedures of the organization. Leadership experts Senn and Childress (1999) state the importance of aligning the strategy, structure, and culture. "Unless culture is properly aligned with business strategies, it is difficult, if not impossible, to implement a new strategic thrust to meet increased competition or changes in the marketplace." Leadership's challenge therefore is to shift the culture into alignment with the strategy and structure.

However, as we shift this culture, we must be very cautious and respectful as the culture that the leader inherits has developed and become entrenched and sacred over time. Greenleaf (1977) shared that one "cannot understand one's involvement in an institution now without a clear sense of the course of events that form the institution's past, out of which grows the mythology that surrounds the record of those events."

Consideration of the culture is critical in assessing and evaluating the effectiveness of teams, the leadership practices that promote effective teams, and the functioning of different models of effective teams that might be used in the workplace. Robbins & Judge (2007, p. 572-573) define organizational culture as "a system of shared meaning held by members that distinguishes the organization from other organizations."

Low-trust cultures do not have the ability to engage in the great effort and difficult work of improvement. High-trust cultures make the extraordinary possible, revitalizing people and giving them the means to succeed under enormously challenging conditions—and the confidence that staying the course will pay off.

It is essential that people understand what makes up an organizational culture, how it is created, sustained and learned. This understanding will enhance our ability to explain and predict the behavior of people at work. Senn and Childress suggest: "All change initiatives must pass through the Jaws of Culture – most get chewed-up, spit out, and forgotten long before they ever accomplish their objectives. The jaws consist of the major cultural barriers that form the ingrained habit patterns of company and individual behavior" (1999, p. 8). Given this statement, it is imperative that organizations become knowledgeable and sensitive to the existing culture.

Changing a culture is a difficult and lengthy process. Bennis, sharing from the work of Bruce Tuckman (2005) describes five different developmental stages of change within a culture. Those stages are referred to as forming, where team members are introduced to the change. Second, storming, where the team begins transitioning from what was to what it aspires to be. Thirdly is the stage called norming. It is at this stage that the team reaches consensus on the "to be" process. Performing is the fourth stage. Here the team has settled its relationships and expectations and is finally at the stage of adjourning where the team is willing to share the process with others. (Smith, M. K. (2005). 'Bruce W. Tuckman – forming, storming, norming and performing in groups, the encyclopedia of informal education.)

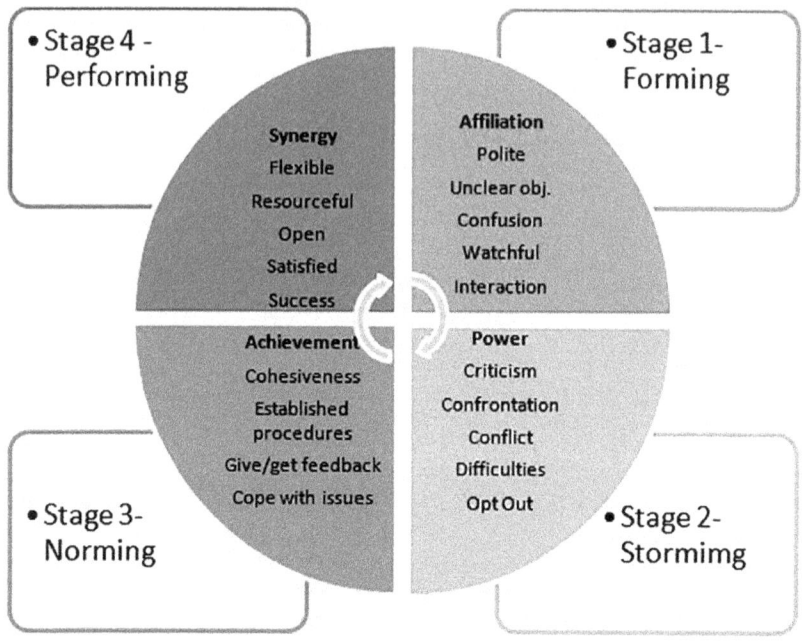

It is important to note that this is most likely not a clear linear process, especially at the storming stage, thus, the origin of the name of this stage. To effectively change a culture, although it may be a much-needed improvement; it is expected there will be many bumps along the road.

I like this description credited to Howard Zinn (1980):

> Revolutionary change does not come as one cataclysmic moment but as an endless succession of surprises, moving zigzag toward a more decent society. We don't have to engage in grand, heroic actions to participate in the process of change. Small acts, when multiplied by millions of people, can transform the world.

I might add; the same holds true in all circumstances with all relationships.

Culture is a common perception that is held by an organization's members. However, it should be expected that individuals with different backgrounds or different levels in the organization might describe the organization's culture differently (Robbins & Judge, 2007, p. 575).

The role of culture acutely influences employee behavior. It is increasingly important in today's workplace. As organizations have widened spans of control and flattened their structure, they have introduced teams, reduced formalization and empowered employees. The shared meaning provided by a strong culture ensures that everyone is pointed in the same direction (Robbins & Judge, 2007, p. 578).

There are many models that describe the role of culture in organizations. Berquist (1992) used the classifications of collegial, managerial, developmental, and negotiating. Cameron and Freeman (1991) used the terms hierarchy, market, clan, and adhocracy to describe their model. As they used the term hierarchy, they refer to the most structured, processed-driven, and controlled culture. Market is results-oriented and competitive. Clan takes the collaborative, family friendly approach with a positive social environment. The final term, adhocracy is described as being flexible, dynamic, innovative, and risk-taking. Deal and Kennedy (1982) use the categories of work-hard, play-hard, tough-guy macho, process, and bet the company.

Although any of the former might be used in this discussion of organizational cultures, this author has chosen the "Four Cultures Model" proposed by William Schneider (1999) which succinctly highlights the central tendencies prevalent in all organizations and can be compared to the other models. I will briefly add some comparison to the Cameron and Freeman model described earlier. Organizational cultures will no doubt be different from one organization to the next; however, all organizations will have similar central tendencies that allow them to be categorized into one of the four culture models. Schneider identified the four cultures in this model as competence, control, collaboration, and contribution.

An organization with a competence culture which is most like the market, results-driven model has more regard for individual contribution than group contributions and believes more in the quantitative aspect than the qualitative aspects. These organizations are highly competitive and driven by achievement. Furthermore, these organizations are constantly asking the question "How?"

An organization with a control culture which is most hierarchal and structured emphasizes building and following plans accompanied by systems, processes and procedures to make them work. The typical question asked in these organizations is "What?"

An organization with a collaboration culture is team-focused, family-friendly and most like the clan culture. The typical question asked in this culture type is "Who?" Organizations in this quadrant win by their in-depth knowledge of customers and other stakeholders.

Finally, organizations with a cultivation culture believe in a lone individual's dream no matter what is said or published. They are dynamic, entrepreneurial, and most like those who advocate for the adhocracy type of culture. At their best, these dreamers deliver dramatic innovation that disrupts the current order and usually win by a total change of the game. Again, I would submit that the most prevalent culture identified in this text is one of collaboration where workers embrace the qualities of loyalty, group cohesion, teamwork, participation, promote mentoring to grow leaders from within the organization. I have a poster on my wall that helps remind me of this. It says in big bold letters: "Who not What; Serve not Dictate; Contribute not Compare; The Common Good not My Ego."

In a school district of only about 600 students and 50 staff members, one of the key people in the administrative office was the business manager. For all payroll issues ranging from salary to benefits and numerous questions about leave, she was the go-to person. However, she wasn't really the go-to person because the people who needed their questions answered were scared to death of her. She was a very knowledgeable and competent employee, but it seemed that every day for her was a bad day and everyone else felt the wrath of her disposition.

As a new superintendent in the district, it didn't take me long to figure out I had a problem that needed to be addressed but I did not want to be biased in my judgments or hasty to take unwarranted action, so I hired a consulting firm to analyze the district climate and operations. The answer that I so highly suspected was revealed loudly and clearly. After several heart-to-heart discussions, she chose to leave before I needed to take action to end her working relationship with the district. Sometimes folks just don't buy into this servant leadership philosophy and if that is the kind of organization you desire than it sometimes requires undesirable actions to take place. It is amazing how the impact of one key person can have such a deleterious effect on an organization. The climate in the district improved immensely with this change in personnel.

I was not able to initiate the same type of action at the Dr.'s office that I found when I moved to a new community. Although the doctor was very competent and had many qualities that exemplified servant leadership, his receptionist and support staff were much lacking in these same qualities. Rather than change the personnel, I changed doctors. I suspect that most of us don't go to the doctor because the visit is something for which we are already looking forward to with great eagerness, so it helps immensely if the staff that are there to welcome you and help you feel at ease actually welcome you and make you feel at ease. I hung on with this doctor for a pretty long time and finally asked myself, why? Since I was the one paying the bill and feeling more negative as time went on I found a more patient-friendly provider and haven't regretted the decision. A continuation of my business and perhaps many others would have been easy. All it takes is a sincere smile.

There are many more in our midst that have much more serious stories to share. They have been victims of this system but despite it are able to overcome the constant battle of one step forward and one step back just to make ends meet. Witness the situation of this young single mother with three children. Her life experiences have been filled with challenges. For example, in only a short period of a couple of months, she was confronted with job losses, automobile problems, health issues, and a myriad of financial challenges. During all of this, she took in others to her already crowded home because they were without housing. Unfortunately, this kindness was not returned with kindness. Rather, items were stolen from the home or ruined and eventually she was forced to abandon her own home or risk her credit and her time with her children.

Each of these unfortunate events was compounded by the lack of enough income but enough income that public assistance was minimal or non-existent. Credit would not be a good option but even if it were it was not even a viable option as at the same time, she had just recently put a bankruptcy behind her.

Throughout many periods of time such as this, overwhelming thoughts of despair abounded with questions of: What do I do now? Where do I go from here? What's going to happen now? And the worst one of all: What is going to happen to us as a family-the kind of family I want for us that I never had for myself?

Somehow, throughout these trials and tribulations she has experienced she has been able to become wise beyond her years, but these experiences have also left some scars that are difficult to diminish even with time. I am also certain that her rich multicultural heritage has enhanced her ability to receive and assist almost anyone in whom she comes in contact regardless of their race, creed, color, or physical appearance or capability. She has an uncanny sense of reading the needs and emotions of others that quickly grows into a common bond not easily initiated and developed by others.

The following short quote from W. Clement Stone (2019) speaks to the amazing strength of this woman.

> "There is little difference in people, but that little difference makes a big difference. That little difference is attitude. The big difference is whether it is positive or negative."

To be an effective leader, you must know when and how to use particular skills and strategies while still being mindful of what is best for the organization and moreover, what is the right thing to do. In their book entitled, "The nature of leadership; Reptiles, mammals, and the challenge of becoming a great leader," White and Prywes (2007) put it this way:

Leadership involves the head and the heart. It is both analytical and interpersonal. Having the range and repertoire to be cold-blooded, rational, and decisive at times, and at other times warm-blooded, nurturing, and participative, and knowing when to be which, is a huge personal challenge. It's right up there with running marathons or learning to play the violin well. Or more accurately, running marathons *and* playing the violin well.

As we reflect on leadership, Schein reminds (2004) us how closely leadership and culture are tied together. Schein states, "Leaders create and change cultures, while managers live within them. High performance will be attributed to organizations, which value trust, empower their people, work collaboratively and connect effectively with the wider community through the involvement of stakeholders external to the organization." In a later book Schein (2009) points out the effort that learning about culture requires. He identifies three layers of culture. The easiest to identify are the visible artifacts but it gets more difficult as one tries to identify the espoused values of the organization and even more difficult to identify the underlying assumptions which include the unconscious, feelings, perceptions, and thoughts that have formed the organizational culture.

Likewise, we must not forget that all of this begins with accepting culture in our own families and homes that bring out the best in them. We do this by seeing and treating others and ourselves not as we are, but as God created us to be (Vallotton & Johnson, 2006). As followers of Christ, we are not only called to serve Him, but also to serve others.

Our work offers us a primary avenue for serving others. For instance, working diligently to process medical insurance claims promptly and accurately may be assisting a young, single parent who urgently needs to have her doctor bills paid. Being attentive to a customer in the clothing department of a retail store may help him make a positive impression on a prospective employer. Even delivering a newspaper on time may help someone who desperately needs to buy an affordable used car that someone has listed in the classified ad section.

It might even be a principal who lights the way to servant leadership. John Halfacre (2011) believed it was the little things more than any major developments or initiatives. He dispelled a number of perceptions of the principal as CEO of the school by doing away with the reserved parking spot, picking up trash around the building, and planning voluntary faculty meetings where the agenda belonged to those who showed up not to him.

I took a slightly different path with faculty meetings when I first became superintendent. Since I didn't live too far from school, about once a month, I invited five or six teachers to be my guest at my home for an extended lunch at my home. Much like Mr. Halfacre, the agenda was theirs. In a year's time, I was able to have each of the staff to my home for this kind of sharing. Again, it was a little thing but it meant a lot. Many individuals who may not have felt comfortable sharing in a larger, more formal staff meeting shared in this small, informal setting. Although, most of the discussions revolved around school issues, we also learned more about each other on a personal level.

To get to know the community a little better and promote the good things that are happening, write a quality newsletter. For less than a cup of coffee, you are able to dress up and go into every home; even those homes where there are no children, but the residents are taxpayers and are part of the community who love to read about the students and staff. While all around us, school construction bonds were failing, ours passed. I believe this regular little visit into everyone's home made a difference.

As is true in most school districts, maintenance staff is in short supply, so I took it upon myself to weed the grounds and plant spring flowers. One of the schools where I was fortunate to serve was located beyond a dead-end cul-de-sac so on the weekends it was a party hot spot. On Monday mornings, I always got to work early to take a tour around the grounds to pick up beer and wine bottles and check for any other signs of inappropriate behavior that I did not want my elementary students to be the first to see.

As a neighborhood elementary school principal there are always opportunities to show you care about the community. One of the communities in which I served was so small that our community didn't show up on maps so we gathered a few interested students together and learned how to get ourselves on the map. There was always fun in being the Master of Ceremonies at the Annual Spelling Bee and the local newspaper was usually quite receptive to receiving copy ready contributions to the paper from the local principal or superintendent. You can also learn a lot about yourself and the people in your community by getting involved in community plays or musicals.

You also must ride one of your regular school route buses. It takes you to a whole different place than where you usually see your students. You see a whole different side of them, and you get a chance to see the importance and the kind of model the school bus driver portrays. It's almost sad to say, but he knows more about the kids then their teacher or principal does. He calls everyone by name and starts and ends their day with a greeting and a smile. Unfortunately, many of our students don't receive this kind of attention before they leave for school in the morning or when they return home in the evening.

It's also fun to share your talents or in my case to show my vulnerability by joining in with the high school students for their karaoke contest or opening the Martin Luther King, Jr. school assembly by singing the National Anthem. I'm sure the young man I invited to accompany me with his trumpet will never forget this event. These are all little things, but they make a big difference and they feel pretty good too.

John Hope Bryant (2009), founder of Operation Hope wrote in his book about leading in a fear-based world: "When you get real with people, when you show real vulnerability, you connect with them, and you move them on a human level. That gives you real power… People meet you where you are."

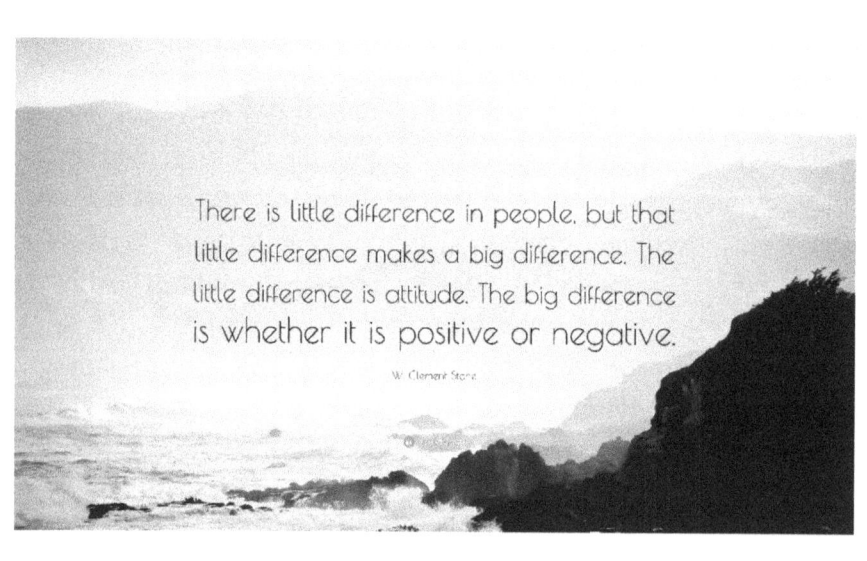

There is little difference in people, but that little difference makes a big difference. The little difference is attitude. The big difference is whether it is positive or negative.

W. Clement Stone

What is the measure of Happiness?

Success is measured in the same ways in the past as it is now—not by wealth, power, property, fame or beauty but by means of determination, perseverance, example, and a positive attitude. We don't have control over the first characteristics, which is really only cosmetic, but we have all the control over the second group, which comes from deep inside of each of us.

A few years back I had the good fortune to make two very enjoyable but contrasting trips to Mexico—one at Christmas time to a poor mission outside of Mexicali and one at another time to the beautiful beaches of Cabo San Lucas. Although, I enjoyed both trips very much, I noticed the beaches of Cabo were filled with people of wealth, power, property, fame, and beauty. Yes, they even had all their tan lines in all the right places. I worked on mine, but I didn't succeed in this area. The people, in the mission near Mexicali, on the other hand, seemed to me to have an even greater love for life and more positive attitudes toward family and things that last more than those with wealth, power and property.

Dr. Robert Spitzer (2000) of the Spitzer Center for Ethical Leadership puts our pursuit of a fulfilling work life and life in general in an outline of four progressive levels in search of happiness. Deep down inside of each of us is the desire to achieve happiness. But what really is happiness and how do we achieve it? According to Fr. Spitzer, the highest level or Level 4 happiness is perfect happiness where the universal human longing for transcendence and perfection is attained. Achieving at this level is a pretty tough challenge for any of us. I have to admit Level 3 is much more within my scope of achievement. This level is directed toward love, truth, goodness, beauty, and unity.

I referred to these same attributes earlier as the ABC's. Affirmation, belonging, and competence encompass most of the attributes spoken to by Spitzer. Regardless of the terminology, the expression of the attributes in this level satisfies and fulfills a very basic hunger that all humans need. It is at this level, where one will find unconditional and reciprocal attention to and from others.

On the other hand, Level 2 is where many of us are but this level is all about me and the present. Unfortunately, this is where we see many of our high-profile athletes and entertainers. They have an incredible opportunity through their fortune and exposure to do so much for others but for whatever reasons seldom choose to do so. Of course, there are wonderful exceptions to this generality such as former NBA player, Dikembe Mutombo who continues to use much of his fortune and notoriety to improve conditions in his homeland, the Democratic Republic of the Congo in Africa.

Level 1 is very basic. It is doing the kind of things that provide immediate but very limited satisfaction. It is derived out of very spontaneous action with little if any reflection on the meaning.

I cannot help but believe that Fr. Spitzer has considered the following example of Jesus in his research and explanation of the Levels of happiness.

Jesus gladdened life around him through His words and example. No words were more frequently on his lips than "be of good cheer" and "be not anxious or afraid." He challenges us to be of good cheer today, even when there is much to discourage us. Whether we are making a speech, performing an audit, sacking groceries, or teaching a class, we can serve as witnesses to our Savior and those around us through the excellence of our work.

Our work provides the setting in which others can see Christ in us. Our lives in the workplace, as well as elsewhere, should reflect the difference God has made in our lives and thereby arouse the curiosity of those with whom we work in the Christ that we know. The next time you start wondering about whether your work matters, consider this: It matters to God; it matters to the people who benefit from the skills and services you offer; and it matters to people who work with you, who over time will recognize the difference in you that only Christ can bring about. It is not necessary to advertise what a great Christian person you are. If you are, people will see it.

Sometimes models are right beneath our eyes, but we don't recognize them because we don't know them. A close high school principal friend of mine said something to the effect that if you spend enough time with anyone, you will find much good in that person. I have met many men in jails and prisons for which I could say this. All of those who are incarcerated are not bad people. They made a mistake or many mistakes. We all do. I read this quote somewhere that speaks to this fact: "I made a mistake. I am NOT a mistake." This is so true. Each of us has unique gifts to share.

Take for instance, Fabian, one of Fr. Gregory Boyle's Homeboys. Boyle (2011) describes him in this way: "His childhood was a mix of a gangster father, mentally ill mother, and no one ever really in their cinco sentidos (right mind) —always high all the time. When he was ten years old or so, his mother was beating him with her high heel, when he sought refuge in the closet. She commenced to beat on Fabian's brother, Michael, and when his brother's screaming stopped, he peeked out of the closet and saw that his mother had wrapped a wire hanger around his neck, and he was turning blue. Fabian flew to her and body-slammed her and wrestled her to the ground. Consequently, no one would have been surprised if Fabian had taken up permanent residence in some state-run, locked down facility."

However, Fabian beat the odds. Due to his involvement with Fr. Boyle and Homeboy Industries, he is a successful, contributing member of society and has a well-paying job and is happily married with three kids.

Another example speaks of the sergeant major that was feared by all until one young private was assigned to him and saw a little bit deeper. Perhaps, this is a poor choice of words. Anyway, one of the first assignments given to the young private by the sergeant major was to clean toilets. Much to the surprise of the private, the sergeant major took him to the latrine and without hesitation, rolled up his sleeves and said, "Here's how you clean a toilet." He got down on his knees in his neatly pressed and cleaned trousers and reached in and scrubbed that porcelain bowl until it shined. Needless to say, this quickly and forever changed the first impression this young soldier had of his leader (Spolsky, 2008, December). You want to know how to get people to do something? Show them! Model it! Be an example!

In an article by Geffrey Kelly (2008), who has done extensive study on the life and writings of Dietrich Bonhoeffer, relates how the poor that we encounter every day in our lives are not just those who are financially poor but just as importantly those who are poor in spirit, including our very selves. He refers to them as Lazaruses from the Lukan story of Lazarus and the rich man. He says, "Lazaruses are those 'who cannot' cope with life, who are often foolish, impertinent, obtrusive, godless, but endlessly in need…" I know I am not devoid of these characteristics, and I see them in others every day, but the question that Bonhoeffer presents is, what do I do about it?

As we work, we must remember with the knowledge that each person we encounter may possess the Lazarus characteristics that Bonhoeffer described or as if we were walking in their shoes as Paul suggested in his analogy of serving a prisoner.

A colleague of mine was asked to do the opening introduction at a Leadership Academy. She shared a wonderful story that illustrated what we sometimes forget as leaders. Briefly her message was that we must not forget to include a good portion of mirth and whimsy in our work. In the book "Furry Logic" (2003), there are numerous great whimsical lessons but one of my favorites says: "You can't stay young forever, but you can be immature for the rest of your like." This is one of my goals. It's a whole lot more fun than taking myself too seriously.

Consider Rose for example: this 87-year young lady who decided to attend college was asked to share some thoughts at an official gathering and so she did. The following short excerpt is part of a much longer description of her address.

> Frustrated and a bit embarrassed she leaned into the microphone and simply said, "I'm sorry I'm so jittery. I gave up beer for Lent and this whiskey is killing me! I'll never get my speech back in order so let me just tell you what I know." As we laughed, she cleared her throat and began:
> "We do not stop playing because we are old; we grow old because we stop playing. There are only four secrets to staying young, being happy and achieving success.
> "You have to laugh and find humor each and every day.
> "You've got to have a dream. When you lose your dreams, you die. We have so many people walking around who are dead and they don't even know it!

At a leadership conference, I heard a young woman from Lima, Peru who earned her doctorate in the United States and is now working for the Washington State University Extension Service as an assistant professor. Karina Gallardo overcame many obstacles to find the success that she has achieved. Despite these obstacles, she makes no excuses and says when someone puts their trust in you, you never betray that trust. You should work hard with high ethics and do it happy.

> "Remember those in prison as if you were their
> fellow prisoners, and those who are mistreated
> as if you yourselves were suffering."
> Hebrews 13:3

Who will you follow?

A Brief Summary of Leadership Styles

Many of the leadership experts of our time have summed up the processes that leaders use with various single verbs. These include: design, foster, invite, persuade, and influence. Leaders typically do things to or for others – for instance, "design learning processes" (Senge and Fullan), "invite others to share authority" Schletchty), "foster mutual respect" (Covey), or engage in "an influence relationship" (Rost) or a "process of persuasion" (Gardner and Sergiovanni).

In a study conducted in 2008 comparing the work of Carl Jung that was used to develop the Myers-Briggs Type Inventory by Katherine and Isabelle Myers and Servant Leadership, the authors (Lewis, Spears, and Lafferty) concluded regarding what they know of Isabelle's motivation for helping to develop the Myers-Briggs typology: "She really wanted to emphasize that we all have gifts that we bring into the world, and for her, the most important aspect of the typology was in helping us recognize those gifts in ourselves, but also, recognizing those gifts in other people. This was not something she was doing to classify people; rather, she sought to help people understand better both themselves and others." Collins (2001) and his team found that "Good to Great" companies developed a strong culture of discipline where the entire company owned responsibility for their "Hedgehog Concept" and all the basics of becoming great. Comparison companies most often had highly disciplined leaders but weren't able to establish a culture that supported that discipline. These findings illuminate the importance of relationships. Levinson (1996) states:

> Relationships are the stuff our lives are made of. They give shape and substance to the life course. They are the vehicle by which we live out – or bury – various aspects of ourselves; and by which we participate, for better or for worse, in the world around us.

It is for this reason that it is critical how a leader demonstrates loyalty, self-sacrifice, and service beyond the call of duty. These actions create a very strong message of what the leader feels is important and necessary. This is the basis for the culture of the organization.

There is a great deal of research, past, present, and ongoing related to leadership styles. This lesson will provide brief overviews of many of these, particularly those styles that fall on the democratic side of the spectrum. These include transformational, moral, charismatic, Covey's two-halves, total, relational, constructivist, fusion, and the soft skills leadership styles. This lesson will also include some of the attributes that lend themselves to these styles of leadership. Other leadership styles have been mentioned earlier, but most that are promoted by this author all have at their core and stem from the first style that will be introduced which is "transformational leadership."

Richard Phillips (1999), in "The Heart of an Executive," shares the following lessons on leadership from the life of King David:

> Direction: The executive must make decisions and communicate effective plans, monitoring and intervening along the way.
> Instilling confidence: His personal presence gave the sheep assurance, calming and moving them forward because of their trust in his watchful care.
> Authority: Followers expect the executive to exercise authority in order to rightly shape behavior, to nudge this one to the left and yank that one back to the right.

Recognition: The shepherd provides recognition and reward to the sheep.

Hope of Belonging: David turns to his own Shepherd with the hope of belonging, of membership in something worthy and meaningful and enduring. It is not David alone whose thoughts rise to such heights. For it is true that people will work for wages and are motivated by recognition and reward. But at the heart of working men and women is the longing--though oft forgotten and sadly despaired of--to participate in something greater than themselves, to belong to a cause that is meaningful and to share in a legacy that endures.

These qualities that Phillips shares from King David's leadership provide a thoughtful segue into the next section where more detail is presented on various styles of transformational or democratic leadership.

What did Burns say about Transformational Leadership?

Most of the leadership styles that fall on the democratic side of the spectrum are offshoots of Burn's transformational leadership style. They include leadership styles that are characterized as moral, charismatic, total, emergent, relational, constructivist, and they possess soft-skills, fusion, mentoring, and will create a legacy. Covey referred to his as the two-halves of leadership. We will also see how Deming's Total Quality Management fits in with the others.

The transformational leaders in these models attempted to achieve a consensus in aligning the individual with organizational interests. The leaders applied a teaching role to their leadership. Burns (1978) asserted when a leader uses this kind of leadership, he can shape, alter, and elevate the motives, values, and goals of his followers. He stated:

> The premise of this leadership is that, whatever the separate interests which persons might hold, they are presently or potentially united in the pursuit of "higher" goals, the realization of which is tested by the achievement of significant change that represents the collective or pooled interests of leaders and followers.

Bass (1997) referred to Mahatma Gandhi and Martin Luther King, Jr. as transformational leaders. Leaders such as these channeled their need for power into socially constructive ways of service to others. Gandhi inspired people through such peaceful efforts as addressing conferences, writing letters, and fasting. His methods attempted to appeal to the goodwill and good reason of the adversary rather than to stir up hatred (Smith, 1964). Like Gandhi, King led his followers through teaching, preaching, and modeling by example. Both men were motivated by love for mankind. They sought justice and fair treatment for all as is espoused in this verse from the Acts of the Apostles:

> "Then Peter began to speak: "I now realize how true it is that God does not show favoritism but accepts men from every nation who fear Him and do what is right."
> Acts 10:34-35

What are some other variations on transformational leadership?

Moral Leadership

Hodgkinson (1991) pointed to a leadership style with a moral emphasis. He emphasized leadership as a humane and moral art whose core problems are philosophical and valuational rather than scientific. He stressed, "Leadership is always a function of value and commitment to organizational value or purpose" (p. 27). A critical aspect of leadership includes the core of values, principles, and fundamental mores.

Hodgkinson further emphasized, "The leader cannot be a cipher or a mere factorum, as is the image of the value-neutered public servant, but must stand for something and, if need be, fall by what value stands for" (p. 36).

Burns (1978), in discussing moral leadership, defined leadership as leaders considering values, motivations, wants, needs, aspirations, and expectations of both leaders and followers. Leadership is therefore inseparable from followers' needs and goals (p. 19).

Sergiovanni (1992) also stressed the moral side of leadership. He said, "The heart of leadership has to do with what a person believes, values, dreams about, and is committed to" (p. 7) Kouzes and Posner (1987) contend leaders who make meaning "breathe life into the hopes and dreams of others and enable them to see the exciting possibility the future holds" (p. 9).

I had the great honor to spend some very precious time with one of the most foremost writers on the topic of ethical leadership. Robert or "Jerry" Starratt (2004) as he prefers to be called was a keynote speaker at a leadership conference where I did some of the planning. After spending hours with him, I found these words from his book "Ethical Leadership" are what he lives and breathes. "Authenticity is the vocation of every human being, the call to bring one's unique possibilities into realization,"

In these words, from Isaiah, we hear this same theme that is referred to here as "moral leadership."

"I, the LORD, have called you into righteousness;
I will take hold of your hand.
I will keep you and will make you to be a covenant for the people
and a light for the Gentiles, to open eyes that are blind,
to free captives from prison and to release from
the dungeon those who sit in darkness."
Isaiah 42: 6-7

Charismatic Leadership

Bass (1990) wrote about charismatic leadership. He noted the attributes that were necessary for this type of leadership. He believed the leader must be a person of strong convictions, determined, self-confident, emotionally expressive, and one with whom followers want to identify (p. 220). However, he didn't feel that a moral component was absolutely necessary for this type of leadership. This explains where some of our political leaders may have many charismatic traits but may possess fewer of the moral traits.

Emergent Leadership

Rogers (1992) wrote about what she called emergent leaders. An emergent would be an enabler, a servant, a collaborator, a facilitator, and a meaning maker (p. 243). She suggested, "Leaders must understand that collaboration, empowerment, multiple perspectives, shared vision, and intuitive wisdom are not just fads in the leadership literature but the result of complex structural changes in the way our society defines itself" (p. 246).

Two-Halves of Leadership

Covey (1996) referred to two halves of leadership. He said the first half is to achieve the private victory; the second half is to get others to join you in your quest to achieve a shared vision (p. 6). In other words, before one can be a successful leader, one must have his own personal life in order. When one's personal life has been attended to, then the leader must have willing followers and co-workers who share the leader's vision. They must involve other people in a shared vision in order to create a supportive environment or culture as was discussed previously. Often, achieving one or the other of these halves is out of the comfort zone of the leader, and the struggle to be effective becomes insurmountable.

Total Leadership

Schwahn and Spady (1998) gave us what they referred to as the total leadership model. Many of the key ingredients share common themes with those identified in the previous models of democratic leadership. They professed, "Total leaders are individuals who embody all of the performance abilities and attributes needed to erect the pillars of productive change and carry out the essential processes that make successful systematic change happen" (p. 17). Schwahn and Spady identified fifteen performance roles of a total leader and categorized these into five major domains. These five domains are identified as authentic, visionary, cultural, quality, and service (p. 29). Total leaders stand on and work from a moral foundation, which includes personal values, organizational values, and principles of professionalism.

Depree (1989) suggested this list of attributes needed by effective leaders. His list included: integrity, vulnerability, discernment, of the human spirit, courage in relationships, sense of humor, intellectual energy and curiosity, respect for the future, regard for the present, understanding of the past, predictability, breadth, comfort with ambiguity, and finally presence. Depree's list contained many of the attributes necessary in exerting power, respecting culture, and gaining and sustaining trust.

> "For as the body is one and has many members, but all
> the members of that one body, being many, are one body,
> so also is Christ. For by one Spirit we were all baptized
> into one body—whether Jews or Greeks, whether slaves
> or free—and all have been made to drink into one Spirit.
> For in fact the body is not one member but many."
> 1 Corinthians 12:12-14

Relational Leadership

Relational leadership involves being attuned to and in touch with the intricate web of inter and intra relationships that influence an organization. That means everyone we serve. Toni Raiten-D'Antonio (2004) writing in her analogy of the Velveteen Rabbit stated: "The best science, philosophy, and theology support the idea that a satisfying life occurs in the long process of establishing and maintaining relationships, talents, meaningful work, and service to others." She also stressed the need for flexibility. Inflexible people break down like mechanical toys because they are unable to respond to serious challenges in creative ways. We must be able to adapt to change. This is aptly illustrated in these actual words from the Velveteen Rabbit (Williams, 1975):

> Real isn't how you are made," said the Skin Horse. "It's a thing that happens to you. When a child loves you for a long, long time, not just to play with, but REALLY loves you, then you become Real." "Does it hurt?" asked the Rabbit. "Sometimes," said the Skin Horse, for he was always truthful. "When you are Real you don't mind being hurt." "Does it happen all at once, like being wound up," he asked, "or bit by bit?" "It doesn't happen all at once," said the Skin Horse. "You become. It takes a long time. That's why it doesn't happen often to people who break easily, or have sharp edges, or who have to be carefully kept. Generally, by the time you are Real, most of your hair has been loved off, and your eyes drop out and you get loose in your joints and very shabby. But these things don't matter at all, because once you are Real you can't be ugly, except to people who don't understand."

When I think of the greatest barriers in my own ability to communicate accurately, I think it is my own self-pride, my own vulnerability, my own desire to have my thoughts and ideas affirmed and reinforced before they are criticized. This gets in the way of moving toward a meaningful discussion. If this small step is not taken, in my mind my own self-worth is being threatened. In fact, it most likely is not a personal affront but I think I am not alone in this common response in conversations. If this reinforcement is not given it limits the conversation from moving on. All a person is able to think about at this point is the attack on his or her character rather than the issue at hand. The ideas or proposals can certainly be altered and should be. Initial ideas that are brought to the table must be modified to meet the needs of the group or the intended audience. However, the thought that the presenter put forward must be validated for the good that is there for trust to be built and productive conversation to ensue.

In an article entitled, "Connect then Lead" from the Harvard Business Review which I believe is one of the premier leadership journals, the authors share their findings on developing relationships and trust as a leader. "Beginning with warmth allows trust to develop, facilitating both the exchange and the acceptance of ideas—people really hear your message and become open to it. Cultivating warmth and trust also boosts the quantity and quality of novel ideas that are produced." (2013, July-August)

I have watched the movie, "Charlie Brown's Thanksgiving many times. I think Charlie Brown is a great leader to his little clan. I couldn't help but think about how the messages of trust, relationships and other important leadership skills are so well portrayed in this movie through the personality and traits of the Peanuts characters. This diverse group of characters is truly a microcosm of many of those groups we serve either as coworkers, constituents, friends, or family. Charlie understood the trials of their middle-class life. He could relate. He lived those trials day after day.

Mark tells us in the following passage how the Son of Man came to make us "Real."

> "You know that in the world the recognized rulers lord it
> over their subjects, and their great ones make them feel the
> weight of authority. But it shall not be among you. Whoever
> would be great among you must be your servant...
> For even the Son of Man did not come to be served
> but to serve and to give His life as ransom for many."
> Mark 10:42-45

Fusion Leadership

Another variation on these models of democratic leadership is fusion leadership. Daft and Lengel (2000) featured this style of leadership which they explained is different than previous hierarchical approaches to leadership. They state that fusion leaders breathe life into dormant subtle forces. These leaders facilitate the development of an overall vision that employees believe in. They appreciate interdependence with others who are also striving to adapt to the environment. The fusion leader successfully empowers others rather than reinforcing hierarchical control, and they build partnerships on shared values and information.

Daft and Lengel define three aspects of fusion leadership. The first aspect can be defined as recognizing one's own subtle leadership gifts, potentials, and passions and acting from them to lead organizational change and improvement. The second aspect shows appreciation for the potential subtle forces in other people and creates fusion processes to help people develop and act on their gifts and potentials. Leaders develop others by showing the way to vision, courage, heart, communication, mindfulness, and integrity. Finally, the third aspect is facilitating organizational change by understanding and using the integration of organizational needs and individual subtle forces through organizational fusion. Considering these three aspects, this style of leadership can be summarized by saying; fusion leadership looks deeply into self and others, seeking to release the vital inner being.

Soft Skills of Leadership

Just as the theme of developing relationships was commonly emphasized in the previous examples, Rowena Crosbie (2005) elaborated on the importance of relational leadership in her discussion of the soft skills of leadership. A leader must balance the process of self-knowledge and self-development with the cultivation of relationships through the development of others. A leader must do all of this while attending to a clear strategy in pursuit of a common goal.

The soft skills of leadership include collaboration/teamwork, communication skills, initiative, people development/coaching, personal effectiveness/personal mastery, planning and organizing, and presentation skills. Aristotle spoke to the three things required for a leader to persuade another person to act. The leader must appeal to logos or logic, appeal to pathos or meaning, and appeal to ethos or trust. In this way a leader is jointly appealing to logic, meaning, and trust. Therefore, a leader must be trustworthy and be able to transmit information that makes sense and evokes desirable emotions.

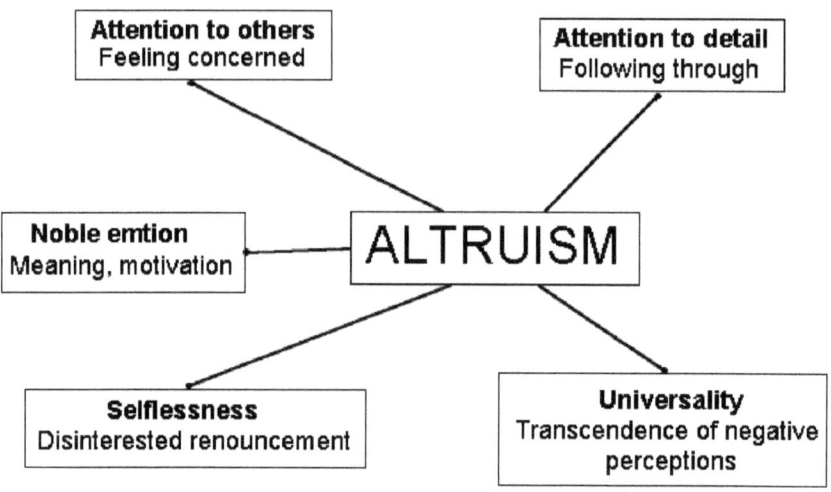

TQM – Total Quality Management

The foundation of total quality management based on the work of Dr. W. Edwards Deming begins with the customer. Quality is defined by the customer and the whole system is devoted to continuous effort at improvement in quality at every step in the process. Managers empower and reward workers who suggest improvements and report concerns with quality.

Dr. W. Edwards Deming was a statistician born in 1900 who grew up in Wyoming and had a passion for quality and sought-after sources and processes to achieve continuous improvement of products. He began his work in earnest is Japan in 1950 but was not recognized in his own country until the 1980's. Critical to the Deming method was the need to base decisions on accurate and timely data. I would submit that his approach relied more on use of a left-brain emphasis then the previous models that I would suggest are more of a right brain approach. Deming advocated the use of a variety of graphic organizers such as charts and diagrams to organize thoughts and information. Dr. Deming's Total Quality Management has been summed up in his "Fourteen Points" and "Seven Deadly Diseases."

The Fourteen Points include the following:

1. Create constancy of purpose for improvement of product and/or service.
2. Adopt the new philosophy.
3. Cease dependence on mass inspection.
4. End the practice of awarding business on price tag alone.
5. Improve constantly and forever the system of production and service.
6. Institute training.
7. Institute leadership.
8. Drive out fear.
9. Break down barriers between staff areas.
10. Eliminate slogans, exhortations, and targets for the workforce.
11. Eliminate numerical quotas.
12. Remove barriers to pride of workmanship.
13. Institute a vigorous program of education and retraining.
14. Take action to accomplish the transformation.

The Seven Deadly Diseases that hinder the process of Total Quality Management are:

1. Lack of constancy of purpose.
2. Emphasis on short-term purpose.
3. Evaluation by performance, merit rating, or annual review of performance.
4. Mobility of management.

5. Running a company on visible figures alone.
6. Excessive medical costs.
7. Excessive costs of warranty, fueled by lawyers that work on contingency fees.

Again, it appears to me that although Deming's method was highly analytical, he valued the importance of relationships that we see in the other transformational models. This can be seen throughout his endorsement of the "Fourteen Points" and obvious aversion for the "Seven Deadly Diseases."

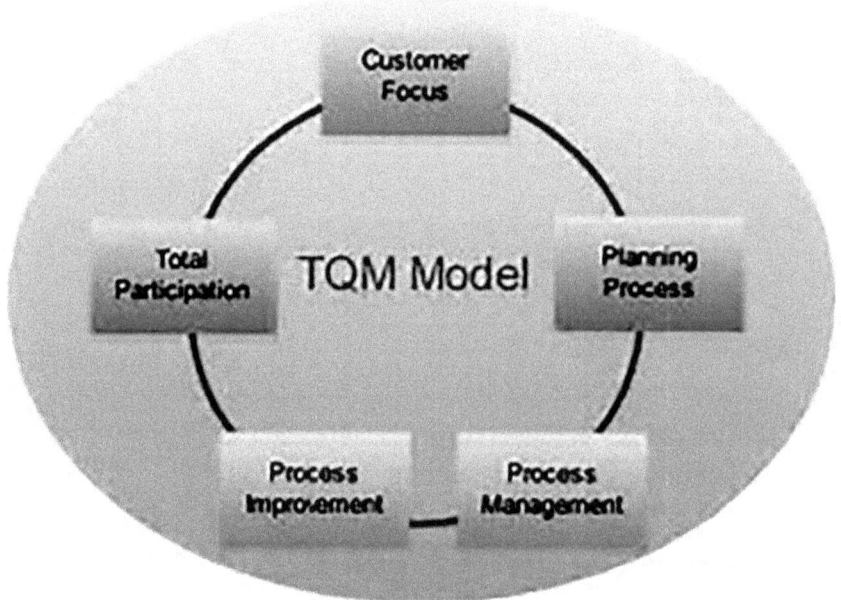

What causes you to follow someone?

Trust — An Essential Component

The key to all of these positive, interdependent relationships is trust. The essential components of trust are benevolence, honesty or integrity, openness, reliability, and competence. These components are achieved through expressing appreciation, honoring agreements, sharing decision making, genuinely talking and listening, demonstrating commitment and dedication, and performing the necessary functions that produce results with high standards and accountability. Tichy and Bennis (2008) tell us, leaders who are trusted honor commitments and promises, their words and behavior match, they are open to reflective backtalk, and they admit errors and learn from their mistakes. An acronym that is helpful to me in remembering how to maintain trust follows:

T – Time
R – Respect
U – Unconditional Regard
S – Sensitivity
T – Touch

But as these words from Ephesians point out, the development of trust is not a one-way process. Trust is a reciprocal process much like the giving of a gift is not truly a gift unless it is received. If both the giver and receiver do not bear with one another in love, patience, and humility than the trust relationship is not complete.

"Be completely humble and gentle; be patient,
bearing with one another in love."
Ephesians 4:2

The Paradox of Leadership

Former President of Whitworth College in Spokane, Washington, William Robinson (2002) suggested consideration of the paradoxes of leadership. It appears followers want the best of both worlds. They want leaders who are authoritative without being authoritarian and forceful without forcing. They want their leader to be common but also heroic. They want a leader who can move deftly between tenderness and cold-bloodedness. This means they should have ice in their veins on matters of principle and morality but have understanding hearts in dealing with human relations. In other words, leaders must know when to use either an approach with a square jaw or a soft heart. Leaders need to be powerful and self-confident but not arrogant and above criticism. They should be visionary but not unrealistic. Leaders do not bring vision, they extract it. This is demanding work but I have heard it said and firmly believe that it is our moral imperative. We must follow the words of Paul to the Galatians.

"Let us not become weary in doing good, for at the proper
time we will reap a harvest if we do not give up."
Galatians 6:9

> ## Leading with mindfulness, selflessness and compassion makes you more human and less leader.
>
> ## It peels off the layers of status that separates you from the people you lead.
>
> ### - The Mind of the Leader
>
> people-equation.com

Constructivist Leadership

Meaning is a prominent theme in current leadership studies. According to Lambert (1995), constructivist leadership enables members of an organization to construct meaning that leads to a common purpose. As members of the organization work collectively, a process can emerge into the formulation of a new meaning of beliefs and culture. An effective constructivist leader presents ideas and opportunities for individuals to construct their own knowledge. He or she creates an environment in which individuals are encouraged to create meaning from experiences and unique perceptions and to act upon acquired knowledge.

Moreover, constructivist leadership is leadership that encourages and facilitates the development of new meaning. Constructivist leaders create and maintain a positive environment in which everyone in the organization is actively engaged in learning, social interaction, sharing of information and self-motivation. These leaders recognize accomplishments of all members of the organization and help to create an environment in which members celebrate others. They use appropriate tools of language and technology to encourage learning and cultivate discussion among others. They maintain the vision of what can be accomplished in an environment based upon informed opinions.

Professional improvement and developing leadership skills for all members of the organization are high priorities. Therefore, leadership in this context can be performed by anyone in the organization because of the full participation of all of those involved.

Roz and Ben Zander (2000) in the "Art of Possibility" speak to these same constructivist ideas. They say:

> The action in a universe of possibility may be characterized as generative, or giving, in all senses of the work—producing new life, creating new ideas, consciously endowing with meaning, contributing, and yielding to the power of contexts. The relationship between people and environments is highlighted, not the people and things themselves. Emotions that are often relegated to the special category of spirituality are abundant here: joy, grace, awe, wholeness, passion, and compassion." They discuss the idea of "leading from any chair.

A leader who feels he is superior is likely to suppress the voices of the very people with whom he must rely on to deliver his vision. The example is given of a conductor of an orchestra who derives his true power from his ability to make other people powerful. Listening for passion and commitment is the practice of the silent conductor whether the players are sitting in the orchestra, on the management team, or on the nursery floor.

Another concept that intrigues me is what they refer to as enrollment. Enrollment is the art and practice of generating a spark of possibility for others to share. So, the practice of enrollment is about giving yourself as a possibility to others and being ready, in turn, to catch their spark. Enrollment is about generating possibility and lighting its spark in others.

The "leader of possibility" invigorates the lines of affiliation and compassion from person to person in the face of the oppression of fear. Any one of us can exercise this kind of leadership, whether we stand in the position of CEO or employee, citizen or elected official, teacher, parent, student, friend or lover. Each person takes responsibility for everything that happens in their life. In this way, there is no blaming or criticism. It takes the "they" out of the equation and replaces it with "we." Each person is part of the solution not the problem. No one person or entity is directed to fix a problem; we are all part of the solution. No one gets to play the role of victim.

In the religious or spiritual setting, homilies are one of the main resources a minister has at his or her disposal to give service. Do the homilies attend to the needs of the assembly? Do they strengthen the faith rather than merely moralize? Do they provide encouragement and hope which leads to prayer and praise and do they promote love and acceptance or are they full of criticism, rebukes, and lectures which demean those who are different than the present audience? – The Priest 2/2011.

Homiletics instructor, Fr. Camillus Foley (2010) tells us that many of our current ministers are clearly not leaders, nor did they intend to be. They have been thrown into a position and a role to which they didn't set out. Their motivation may have been to perform pastoral ministries, minister to the poor, or teach religious education and yet they have been placed in leadership roles. There is nothing wrong with this, but we still need new leadership in our churches to spread the message to love one another in a way that people will embrace it and act upon it.

Guilt trips and man-made denominational rules don't cut it anymore. People who study scripture and spend quiet time in prayer can see through the hypocrisy. Inbred upbringing in a particular denomination does not hold the same attraction or obligation as it did in the past. Dr. Dan Mosely, teacher of preaching and leadership says it well. He says, "People are hungry. The pews of our churches are peopled with souls hungry for something to nourish their lives and give them courage to live more fully and abundantly.

Preaching that transforms us is that which evokes the presence of healing, loving, and powerful resources from within us. Powerful and transformative preaching is not as much about the information we can communicate as it is about the presence that we can facilitate." (2008, Oct-Dec)

As we leave our place of worship, we ought to be able to echo the following words by Calvin Miller:

> Promise me, that I, who am riddled by inferiority, will at last believe in myself. Promise me that after your words, I will be able to scale the icy walls of my fears and with God's help plant his mighty flag on the summit of all my doubts. Promise me that I at last will know who I am and what I was meant to achieve. Promise all this and you shall have first my ear…and then my soul.

It is this kind of hunger that is filled when we reach out to our co-workers with the kind of love that Luke speaks of in the following passage:

> "The Spirit of the Lord is on me,
> because he has anointed me
> to preach good news to the poor.
> He has sent me to proclaim freedom
> for the prisoners and recovery of sight for the blind,
> to release the oppressed,
> to proclaim the year of the Lord's favor."
> Luke 4:18-19

In this lesson entitled, "Who will you follow?" various transformational or democratic styles of leadership and those who espoused this type of leadership have been briefly examined. Included were James McGregor Burns' Transformational Leadership; and Hodgkinson, Sergiovanni and others who speak to the importance of Moral Leadership. Bernard Bass advocated Charismatic Leadership and J.L. Rogers shared insights regarding Emergent Leadership. Stephen Covey referred to the Two-Halves of Leadership and Dr. W. Edwards Deming suggested a model he referred to as TQM or Total Quality Management. Brief comments were shared about what Schwann and Spady referred to as Total Leadership and Toni Raiten-D'Antonio provided an example of Relational Leadership from the children's classic book, The Velveteen Rabbit by Williams. We even pondered an example from Charlie Brown. An explanation of Fusion Leadership was shared from the work of Daft and Lengel. Rowena Crosbie emphasized the theme of relationships in describing the Soft Skills of Leadership and the importance of constructing meaning and creating a common purpose was shared from Linda Lambert's work in the area of Constructivist Leadership.

Do the Least of Those Served Grow as Persons?

Thus far, a variety of leadership theories, styles, and attributes have been discussed. Many of these have very close similarities to servant leadership but this lesson will focus most specifically on the style of leadership made known by Robert Greenleaf as servant leadership. Robert K. Greenleaf is recognized as the father of servant leadership. Greenleaf retired from AT&T in 1964 as Director of Management Research. That same year, he founded an international, nonprofit organization known as the Center for Applied Ethics. In 1985, the Center for Applied Ethics became the Robert K. Greenleaf Center for Servant Leadership. It is located in Indianapolis, Indiana. Greenleaf published his first writing on servant leadership at the age of 60. Greenleaf viewed the period between the ages of 60-75 as his most productive and it was during these years that he taught his concepts of servant leadership. He wrote extensively and served as consultant to organizations such as the Ford Foundation, the Lily Endowment, and the American Foundation for Management Research, the Mead Corporation, and even the government of India. Greenleaf died in 1990 at the age of 86.

The event that crystallized Greenleaf's thinking came in the 1960s, when he read Hermann Hesse's short novel "Journey to the East"—an account of a mythical journey by a group of people on a spiritual quest.

The central character of "Journey to the East" was a man named Leo. Leo was one of the servants on the journey. He helped to carry the luggage and was assigned other rather menial tasks. This unaffected man had something so pleasing, so unobtrusively winning about him that everyone loved him. He did his work gaily, usually sang or whistled as he went along, was never seen except when needed -- in fact an ideal servant... This servant Leo worked in a very simple and natural manner. He was especially friendly in an unassuming way. After reading this story, Greenleaf concluded that its central meaning was that the great leader is first experienced as a servant to others, and that this simple fact is central to the leader's greatness. True leadership emerges from those whose primary motivation is a deep desire to help others.

I had the pleasure of meeting a similar Leo character while serving as a monitor at a men's emergency shelter in our local community. Juan was allowed to show up a little later than others as he was either helping family or assisting in one of the daytime missions in the area. He was the last to leave the next morning as he quietly went about tidying up and cleaning after everyone else had left. I never saw anyone give him any direction. He just saw what needed to be done, got it done, and then he got on his bike to ride to the mission to work. None of this gave him any income, he just did it. I did notice he carried his Bible when he arrived and when he left but I never saw him proselytizing, at least not in words, he did it all by his actions.

Greenleaf was raised in the Judeo-Christian tradition as practiced through Quaker beliefs. While Quakers do not adopt religious beliefs as dogmas, their societal framework supports religion as a life to be lived and an experience to be shared. Their values support the practice of building a better society. The Quaker sense of the presence of God is viewed as a catalyst to action, to alleviate suffering and create a better society. The Quaker belief that there is good in everyone and there is God in everyone is evident in Greenleaf's articulation of servant leadership. Within the Quaker belief system, the leader is to support a community where the leader is committed to the enrichment of the lives of each member of that community.

My thoughts regarding servant leadership parallel very closely those expressed by Banuelos (2003). She stated:

> Servant Leadership challenges our old ideas of managing people and events. It is not linear, nor does it have boundaries. It is a way of honoring gifts that people bring and skills and talents they have rather than always looking to put something into them that doesn't exist. Servant leadership requires that we listen not only with our ears but also with our hearts. It requires we bring our souls to the table and expose our true selves so others can do the same. It requires true honesty and the setting aside of self-interest (p. 1).

As a leader in public schools since 1982, I have taken my calling and responsibility of leading very seriously. In education we are entrusted with the world's future. I had the honor and enjoyment of trying to bring out the skills and talents in all of those we serve. It was at least as far back as 1982 when I came across a small entry in a newsletter that talked about a new kind of leadership. I saved the contents of this brief article to this day, and it gave me the realization that we can lead in such a way that all participants grow in the process. It spoke of uniting people and giving them direction using a new kind of leadership called servant or transformational leadership. A servant leader guides his or her team members, utilizing a style of leadership based upon such values as cooperation, support and the encouragement of leadership qualities in all members. In a much more recent article, Youngs (2007, April) illustrates very graphically the factors of servant leadership practice.

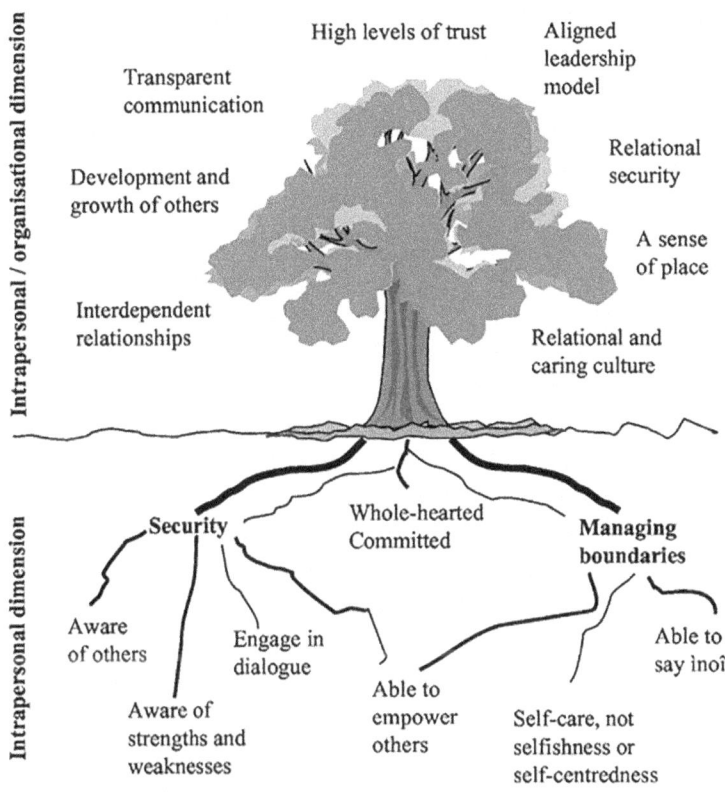

Figure 2. The Internal and External Factors of Servant Leadership Practice.[29]

Enter Pope Francis, who has made the servant leadership message his mantra and is certainly modeling the components of figure 2 above. Born in Buenos Aires, Argentina, on December 17, 1936, Jorge Mario Bergoglio became Pope Francis on March 13, 2013, when he was named the 266th pope of the Roman Catholic Church. Bergoglio, the first pope from the Americas, reportedly took his papal title after St. Francis of Assisi of Italy. Prior to his election as pope, Bergoglio served as archbishop of Buenos Aires from 1998 to 2013. He is the first pope from the Americas. Pope Francis recently passed away on April 21, 2025. He has been succeeded by Pope Leo XIV on May 8, 2025. He is the first Pope from the United States; South Chicago, Illinois.

It would be accurate to say he has shaken the world with his openness and love for all people. He has proven to be an ambassador to the poor and the disenfranchised. He continually preaches a message of love and forgiveness rather than guilt and damnation. Pope Leo XIV (Cardinal Robert Prevost) is expected to follow in the footsteps of Pope Francis.

Why Should One be a Servant Leader?

Tarr (1995), in one of his selections pertaining to leadership, asked: "Why should one be a servant leader?" (p. 81). He gave four reasons. The first was simply, it works. He stated that excellent companies attempt to satisfy the needs and anticipate the wants of their customers. Secondly, servant leadership reinforces the nature of one's profession and calls upon its more noble instincts. He emphasized the role of servant is to bring people together, to collaborate, to co-sponsor, to break down walls, and to assist in the learning process. Thirdly, servant leadership is action oriented. There is always something to do when you focus on others first. Finally, servant leadership is a commitment to the celebration of people and their potential (pp. 82-83).

Whether a person is an administrator, coach, or committee chairperson, the servant leader always keeps the community-held goal in full view of the team. Victor Frankl (1968) noted: "Everyone has his own specific vocation or mission in life; everyone must carry out a concrete assignment that demands fulfillment. Therein he cannot be replaced, nor can his life be repeated, thus, everyone's task it unique as his specific opportunity."

Greenleaf (1977) described it in this way:

> It begins with the natural feeling that one wants to serve, to serve first. Then conscious choice brings one to aspire to lead…The difference manifests itself in the care taken by the servant—first to make sure that other people's highest priority needs are being served. The best test, and difficult to administer, is: do those served grow as persons; do they, while being served, become healthier, wiser, freer, more autonomous, more likely themselves to become servants? And, what is the effect on the least privileged in society; will they benefit, or at least, not be further deprived? (pp. 13-14)

Larry Spears (1995) was the former Executive Director of the Greenleaf Center. (Kent M. Keith was the former Executive Director) Spears compiled ten particulars that assist in identifying leaders who embrace the philosophy of servant leadership. These particulars were listening, empathy, healing, awareness, persuasion, conceptualization, foresight, stewardship, commitment to the growth of others, and building community (pp. 3-6).

Spears (1997) defined each of the ten particulars as critical for the servant leader to possess. In the next ten lessons, each of these particulars will be discussed. I am convinced they will also compliment the following principles of servant leadership:

- Commitment to the diversity of human gifts
- The concept of covenantal relationships
- The ability to both yield and follow
- Concept of offering opportunities, not obligations
- Willingness to assume a position of humility
- Deep respect for the values of people
- Intense courage of one's convictions
- Passionate advocate for human dignity and the common good
- Infectious optimism

- Ability to offer hope in the face of fear
- The wisdom of experienced knowledge
- The ability to gain and sustain trust
- Ability to lead in a nourishing fashion
- Appreciation of the inner direction of others

Ervin (1997) pointed out that many of the same qualities are written about in the second chapter of the book of Philippians (New International Version). Paul wrote that servanthood should include living with humility, obedience and by example. Example is a very critical component as it enables people to follow, even when they don't clearly understand the directions or instructions. Some would say this servant attitude leaves a person open to vulnerability. However, Ervin argued that would not be servanthood, but servitude. Servanthood is a conscious choice to do that which causes others to benefit. Servitude, on the other hand, is a forced manipulation.

Not that I believe it was the intended message of the text from John 13 where Jesus washed the feet of his disciples, but can you imagine how dirty these feet might have been. I never gave it much thought but while reading from a story about the Jews being sent to remote places during World War II; one of the characters calls out to his mother about the appearance of the feet of the people in the remote Italian community where Jews have been sent. The feet were so encrusted with dirt that they had the appearance of hardened leather. Even closer to home and more recently, one of the young men who is a frequent visitor at one of the local Homeless Shelters asked if he could get a pan of water to wash his feet. My partner for the evening monitoring pleasantly obliged and the man went off to the men's room to wash his feet. Not too long after, my partner returned to the restroom to check on the man and found the stench so great that he had to leave until the job was done and the room could be aired out. The point again is that in both of these instances the dirty feet were the result of dust, dirt, mud, and poor shoes without frequent opportunities to wash. So, I am thinking Jesus's job of washing the feet of his disciples may have been quite a bit more poignant than I had previously envisioned.

This same reading about the Jewish people, made me also question why the Jews were a target of such blatant abuse and exclusion more than anyone else. Not that it would help justify the actions taken against them, but my knowledge of history is not astute enough to know where and why it all originated. Jewish people continue to struggle with a sense of belonging, not as Jews but as a member of any particular nation. Rabbi Reines (2009-Jan-Feb) recalls an incident where Jewish composer, Herman Berlinski sought to flee Nazi-occupied France for America. The French security officer was confounded by Berlinski's documentation of his national identity. Berlinski presented a German birth certificate, a Polish passport because he was a Polish citizen, documentation of his father's American citizenship, and his own military documentation of serving in the French Foreign Legion. For most Jewish people who have been forced to leave country after country, the one firm identity they have to hold on to is that they are Jews.

Why do you Choose to go to the Places you go?

Service First

Sype and Frick (2009) tell us, "A servant-leader wants to make a difference for others and to have an impact on their lives. They will sacrifice their own self-interests for the sake of others. They choose "to lead as a servant, to risk mistakes and achievements." Fullan (2003) asks directly what is motivating you to make a difference. It's all about relationships.

Consider the Subaru guy for example. I wasn't desperate for a car but was really attracted to the Subaru Baja. It had enough room to carry people in the back seat plus it had a small pick-up area big enough to take a little rubbish to the dump. I found what I wanted but was not getting the kind of attention and service that showed me that the young salesman wanted to sell me a car. The bottom line was; I wasn't getting service. I was on my way out the door when the owner of the business for more than twenty years called me aside and gave me some SERVICE. He provided this gracefully enough that he didn't humiliate the young salesman but moreover modeled for him how to treat customers.

Having worked in the food and beverage industry for many years myself, I am always on the lookout for those restaurant employees who provide that extra bit of the "WOW" factor. As I'm thinking about this, I'm on my way to work listening to sports' talk radio and one of the hosts is bragging on and on to the other host about this great tavern in New York City where he took his wife for her birthday. He can't say enough about the terrific service. It really is why we go where we go. As soon I could get to a computer I searched for reviews on "The Gramercy Tavern" in New York City. The reviews were even more complimentary than this talk show host had shared. One reviewer commented: "Wow! Just wow! I love their service. They know what professionalism is." Another added: "The wait staff was attentive, candid, and funny." Well, that's New York City; this is central Washington State but Jackie also is one of these exceptional servers. In addition to her great service, efficiency and sense of humor one of the qualities that impresses me most about her is how she treats her fellow employees who help her be so successful. She never fails to give them a very sincere "thank you!' and she gives them a healthy share of her tips. These little things enhance the positive atmosphere wherever she works because everyone is being appreciated, not only the guests but also the employees.

Randy Pausch, author of the Last Lecture, shared this same philosophy of giving gratitude. Randy was a research professor with a team of fifteen researchers. When he was awarded with tenure, he took all fifteen to Disneyland with him. His message to all of us is: "Show Gratitude." After working and playing through all of these experiences, do you think all of those involved were more committed to their work and to each other? You bet!

A reminder of five practices that help leaders serve others are the following actions:

S – See the Future
E – Engage and Develop Others
R – Reinvent Continuously
V – Value Results and Relationships
E – Embody Values

People Listen and Sometimes Hear

Listening and Reflection

Cartoon character, Charlie Brown, seems to exemplify being either misunderstood or not taken seriously for what he does say. In just one of many such comic strips, Lucy asks Charlie Brown if he can take a little friendly advice. Being the great guy that he is; he says, "Why of course, I'm not above that sort of thing at all; a little friendly criticism can always be helpful to a person. What is it you wanted to say?" Lucy, consistent with her character replies, "You're kind of stupid."

In sharp contrast is children's TV host, Fred Rogers (2003). He says, "In times of stress, the best thing we can do for each other is to listen with our ears and our hearts and be assured that our questions are just as important as our answers."

This is one of my favorite quotes from "The Art of Racing in the Rain" (2008) by Garth Stein. It really is true. We can learn a lot from dogs.

> "Here's why I will be a good person. Because I listen. I cannot talk, so I listen very well. I never deflect the course of the conversation with a comment of my own. People, if you pay attention to them, change the direction of one another's conversations constantly."

Dogs are great examples in other ways, as well. On a trip to the Oregon Coast, I found a "Doggie Daycare" where I could leave our little dog Gracie. I had never been to one of these types of places previously, so I didn't know what to expect. What I found was a large indoor playground where all dogs were out to recess. Like little children, they all played with each other like great friends. It didn't matter what size, breed, color or shape. They all just got along.

On another occasion, my son and daughter in law brought their newborn to our house. There was an immediate attraction from the newborn to Gracie. Gracie guarded the new baby as if it were her own pup. How did she know to do this? Where did the dogs in the daycare learn their social skills?

> Rick Rigsby (2006) in "Lessons from a Third Grade Dropout," notes: "As you express kindness by choosing to share deeds of encouragement, gentleness, and politeness, the entire organization, will reap the rewards." The dogs in the daycare certainly reaped the rewards by sharing positive social skills.

These short little vignettes lead us to our discussion of listening, the first of the necessary particulars of servant leadership. Servant leaders must demonstrate a deep commitment to listening intently to others. They must seek to listen receptively to what is being said and even what is not said. Listening also encompasses getting in touch with one's inner voice during times of reflection, and seeking to understand what one's body, spirit, and mind are communicating. Listening honestly and openly has a lot to do with integrity. (Spears, 1997)

Hodgkinson (1991) pointed out how important the process of reflection or listening to one's own inner voice is to leaders. He referred to the term "praxis." Praxis is a term conceived by Aristotle to describe ethical actions guided by purposes, morals, emotions, and values, as well as facts. Hodgkinson stated: 'Praxis clearly applies to all leadership, but it implies a duality in action, two "moments": one of consciousness or reflection in the first moment, and one of action and commitment in the second moment" (p. 43).

Greenleaf (1998) admitted:

> "Meditative intervals have been very important to me – both long ones and short ones. It has sometimes been crucial, in the heat of controversy, to withdraw into silence for just a few seconds so that the creative processes can function. For a big idea to evolve; I have found that a big chunk of meditative time is required."

Covey in his Seven Habits (1989) pointed out that this type of listening is an attempt to put oneself into another person's shoes, and view it from her viewpoint, and be able to state in our own words to that person what they have told us, and essentially have her say, "You are right. That is exactly what I said."

A leader that I worked with not too long ago does that with great expertise. She never moves forward in a conversation until she has done exactly as Covey has suggested. You know without a doubt that you have been heard and heard accurately. To be able to get to this point is truly the ultimate in terms of listening. Then you have really understood where they are coming from.

There is perhaps no greater gift than being listened to and heard. Those who are able to give you the attention where you are convinced you are heard and understood are truly meeting a very great need.

Jaworski (1996), in his leadership guide "Synchronicity," said: "Just being able to be there for others and to listen to them is one of the most important capacities a leader can have" (p. 66). Jaworski was inspired by Greenleaf's servant leadership theory when he first began thinking of his own leadership. He submitted that leaders must have a mind shift away from a world make up of things to a world that's open and primarily made up of relationships. Listening is a critical component of successful relationships. Listening calls forth the best in people by allowing them to express what is within them. Jaworski expressed, "If someone listens to me say what I am feeling, then my feelings are given substance and direction, and I can act" (p. 66).

The art of listening places both the speaker and listener in the position of vulnerability. It is through listening that we can make our genuine presence known, that we can convey an attitude of caring involvement and that matters of the heart and mind can be synergistically communicated. Listening allows us to uncover interests, fears, and new options. Listening allows us to explore ambiguity rather than shun it. Listening allows us to respect difference, and to look for ways to go on together (Forester, 1989). The art of listening is indeed both an act of the will and a manifestation of love (Peck, 1978). John Maxwell states:

> If you're going to connect, people need to know that you understand them. They need to sense that you're there for them. Good communicators understand that people do things for their own reasons, not for the reasons of the person doing the talking. Accordingly, they focus on the listeners' needs not their own."

As a leader, I am not eager to be like the school principal in the cartoon that quips: "I connected a food processor to my computer, in case I have to eat my words." It would be much more appropriate to follow the advice of Paul to the Ephesians.

> "Do not let any unwholesome talk come out of your mouths, but only what is helpful for building others up according to their needs, that it may benefit those who listen."
> Ephesians 4:29

Make **EYE CONTACT**

Be an **ACTIVE** listener!

FOCUS ON what is being said

FACE the speaker

REPEAT BACK what you heard

TELL THE SPEAKER if you understand or don't understand

NOD your head

ASK questions

Wait for the speaker to stop **BEFORE SPEAKING**

Keep **HANDS** and **FEET STILL**

IGNORE distractions

Who's Got Your Back?

Empathy

Empathy is the next element the servant leader must consider. Empathy causes the servant leader to accept and recognize others, especially co-workers, for their special gifts and unique spirits. One must assume the good intentions of coworkers and not reject them as people, even when forced to reject their behavior or performance.

According to Wheatley (1994), leadership is making the shift from placing the importance on the work, to placing the importance on the workers. She noted, "Managers have recently been urged to notice that they have people working for them." Each person has strong desires for recognition and connectedness. Wheatley admonished, "We cannot hope to influence any situation without respect for the complex network of people who contribute to our organizations" (p. 144).

Morrie in "Tuesdays with Morrie," (Albom, 1997) advised: "Be compassionate and take responsibility for each other. If we only learned those lessons, this world would be so much better a place. We must love each other, or we will die" (p. 163).

Quaker Pastor Philip Gulley (1998) maintains some people build boats and others build people. It starts and is modeled by the mother or father whose idea of a good time is reading to the children; or the social worker who drives a client to the doctor on his day off; or the teacher whose deepest joy is that special moment of "Aha!" These people builders rise each day at dawn, say their prayers, and go forth to build their little corner of the kingdom. If Tuesday is bad, they trust Wednesday will be better. They are patient. There is no rush. They are building people and that takes time (p. 94).

Empathy and collaboration are enormous strengths and qualities of a leader who exhibits qualities of transformational leadership. Leaders who lack these strengths tend to react to change defensively and ineffectively. Defensiveness can block a team's effectiveness, and it must be identified and worked out (Senge, 1990, p. 254).

Billy Graham (1999) shared an unfortunate reality in saying that if a man were sent to Mars to report earth's major business; it is likely he would have to say that war was the earth's chief industry. He would have to report that the nations of the world spend the majority of their efforts vying with each other in a race to see who can make the deadliest weapons and amass the biggest arsenal of these weapons. He would say that people on planet earth are too quarrelsome to get along with each other and too selfish to live peacefully together.

Basic emotional needs that all of us hunger for are respect, recognition, belonging, affirmation, reconciliation, and approval. The life of Jesus reflected these qualities of servant leadership long before current leaders began to embrace the principles; Wright (2007) described the life of Jesus in this way:

"He ate with sinners, healed people, fed them, faced down angry mobs, and confronted religious big shots. He taught about loving enemies, sharing with the poor and blessings that do not depend on money. He gave us a different way to be alive—not just a different way of living, but a different reality of being. Instead of muddling along with a normal set of human concerns and goals about getting ahead and providing for old age and all that, every action was shaped to show God's true will for humanity" (pp. 15-16).

It is unfortunate but the following quote by Gandhi bears a lot of consideration when we look at the model Jesus portrayed: "If Christians would really live according to the teachings of Christ, as found in the Bible, all of India would be Christian today." He truly was a model for the principle of empathy. Mahatma Gandhi is widely considered the father of India, a great influencer, and the symbol of peace.

Why is it we so often we place so much dignity to briefcases, white collars and academic robes, while denying it to lunch pails, muddy overalls and greasy caps?

We have recently lost a great world leader in Pope Francis, not merely a religious leader, his leadership impacted the whole world. He truly walked the talk and showed by his example how the world he envisioned could coincide with the world where Jesus was described in the above quote from Wright.

Doesn't Anyone Know how I Feel?

Healing

One of the great strengths of servant leadership is the potential for healing oneself and others. Learning to heal is a powerful force for transformation and integration. Servant leadership focuses first on the healing of the leader through a search for wholeness, completeness, and connectivity. Greenleaf wrote: "There is something subtle communicated to the one who is being served and led if, implicit in the compact between the servant-leader and led is the understanding that the search for wholeness is something that they have."

Dr. Shine (2014, W. Murphy) a shoeshine man at Boston's Logan Airport has found this understanding. He's about 65 years old and has MS and must use a walker to get around. But you see, he doesn't think of himself as much as a shoeshine man or as a disabled person as he does a psychiatrist who works his magic to find the spark inside people so that when they leave him, they can shine more brightly on their own. As Dr. Shine shines your shoes, he tries to find out how to bring the shine out in each of those that come to him. He refers to his shoeshine stand as his office. This humble old man with a disability improves his outlook on life while he improves the outlook of others. Wow!

Creating a healing atmosphere by demonstrating compassion and care in a timely fashion is critical in helping staff to deal with difficult times. It is important to employees that they know their needs are given high priority. This portion of a piece from "one tree hill" describes so well what kind of compassion and caring people are looking for in healing.

> Sometimes it's easy to feel like you're the only one in the world who's struggling, who's frustrated, or unsatisfied, or barely getting by. That feeling is a lie. And if you just hold on, just find the courage to face it all for another day. Someone or something will find you and make it all okay. Because we all need a little help sometimes.... Someone to help us hear the music in the world, to remind us that it won't always be this way. That someone is out there. And that someone will find you.

Rachel Remen tells us:

> "Healing may not be so much about getting better, as about letting go of everything that isn't you—all of the expectations, all of the beliefs—and becoming who you are.
>
> Wounding and healing are not opposites. They're part of the same thing. It is our wounds that enable us to be compassionate with the wounds of others. It is our limitations that help us to find other people or to even know they're alone.

Seitz and Pepitone (1996) explained that servant leaders are motivated to build a better, more caring society. They wrote, "Servant leaders thrive on watching and helping others grow and they acknowledge that it is necessary to develop a component of personal and spiritual growth within the individual.

Jesus Christ's principles and actions serve as the best example of servant leadership. He led by claiming the first two verses of Isaiah 61 as His mission. As quoted from the Jerusalem Bible: "He has sent me to bring good news to the poor, to build up hearts that are broken, to proclaim liberty to the captives…and to comfort all those who mourn."

Robinson (2002) concluded: "The essential leadership qualities for the 21st Century will be portrayed by leaders who move humbly among all people until it is time to step forward with unshakable confidence, whose selflessness energizes all those around them, who know that good decisions come from good information, who can knit heart and mind into a compelling mandate, whose uncompromising goodness quietly beckons the most valuable gift that is trust and who are able to find a balance where both personal and professional desires are fulfilled" (p. 26).

The following poem written by a man in a homeless shelter to the staff and volunteers speaks volumes of how little acts of kindness make a huge difference to those who receive the acts.

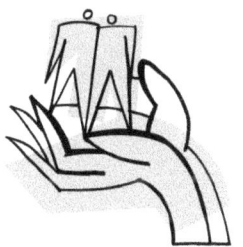

> It's not the great Cathedral
> Or the High Mass softly sung.
> It's not the beaded rosary,
> Or solemn church bells rung.
>
> It's not the bed and shower;
> It's not the evening meal;
> It's not this warm old building
> That makes God's love so real.
>
> It's just the simple kindness
> You show to every man;
> The way you help the drunkard
> And give him strength to stand
>
> It's in the smile you give us
> No matter how rude we seem;
> It's in your calm, your patience
> That we learn what loving means.
>
> We see the God within you;

His Love is in this place.
We see Jesus walk among us;
And He wears your smiling face.

--Charlie Lambert

In like manner, the following two short passages speak poignantly to the need to open our hearts to all.

"For if a man with gold rings on his fingers and in fine
clothes comes into your assembly and a poor person in
shabby clothes also comes in, and you pay attention to the
one wearing the fine clothes and say, 'Sit here, please,' while
you say to the poor one, 'Stand there," or "Sit at my feet,'
Have you not made distinctions among yourselves
and become judges with evil designs?"
James 2: 2-4

From "A Touching Place" by John Bell

Feel for the people we most avoid.
Strange or bereaved or never employed;
Feel for the women, and feel for the men
fear that their living is all in vain.

Feel for the parents who lost their child,
feel for the woman whom men have defiled.
Feel for the baby for whom there's no breast,
and feel for the weary who find no rest.

Feel for the lives by life confused.
Riddled with doubt, in loving abused;
Feel for the lonely heart, conscious of sin,
which longs to be pure but fears to begin.

Why Weren't You There When I Needed You?

Awareness and Perception

One of the greatest writers on leadership of all time, John Gardner (1990), revealed one of the most puzzling truths regarding awareness. He stated:

> The most gifted leaders understand that the needs of people cannot be fully plumbed by asking them what they want or why they want it. One of the deepest truths about the cry of the human heart is that it is so often muted, so often a cry that is never uttered. To be sure, there are needs and feelings that we express quite openly; lying deeper are emotions we share only with loved ones, and deeper still the things we tell no one. We die with much unsaid. It is strange that members of a species renowned for communicative gifts should leave unexpressed some of their deepest yearnings, their smoldering resentments, their worries and secret hopes, their longings to serve a higher purpose.

General awareness, and especially self-awareness, strengthens the servant leader. Making a commitment to foster awareness can be frightening because one never knows what one may discover. As

Greenleaf observed, "Awareness is not a giver of solace—it's just the opposite." As a new leadership team, we refer to what we may discover, as one more stone we have turned over. However, one cannot shirk the responsibility of leadership by avoiding the kind of awareness that illuminates current challenges and challenges of the past that have been overlooked or left unaddressed. To achieve the kind of awareness and perception that uncovers these stones, leaders must make every effort to be visible and involved so they understand the workings of the entire organization.

Spears (1995), in describing this element stated, "Awareness aids one in understanding issues and values. It lends itself to being able to view most situations from a more integrated, holistic position." (p. 4).

Greenleaf maintained that a primary quality of leadership is one that can endure a sustained breadth of awareness, so the leader knows at all times what is occurring throughout the organization. Leaders who stay in their office and never come out to have any contact with employees are ineffective. They must know their organization and know what is really going on.

A leadership team like the one mentioned above that spends the majority of their time in their offices never believed that in their first year with the organization they would deal with the issues of which they became aware. Such issues as employee absences without giving notice, employee use of drugs and alcohol during work hours, gambling addictions, the use of tobacco and other substances at the workplace, developing relationships at the workplace that grow into sexual activities at the workplace, inappropriate staff and student relationships, middle management misappropriating funds and seemingly hiding their knowledge of this inappropriate use, lack of enforcement of expected employee duties, and giving away public funds and property are just the beginning of what being aware has exposed. With this beginning, we could only guess what more was to come. They were only halfway through their first year.

Our challenges reminded me of one of my favorite poems, "If" by Rudyard Kipling. A few lines that speak to awareness and perception are: "If you can keep your head when all about you are losing theirs and blaming it on you…If you can meet with Triumph and Disaster and treat those two imposters just the same…If neither foes nor loving friends can hurt you; If all men count with you…Yours is the Earth and everything that's in it."

This is the frustrating side of being aware and perceptive but there are as many instances that bring solace and joy.

We live in a city, state, country, and world where we have no real idea how neighbors less than 200 miles away actually live and what their needs are. One of our nearest national neighbors is Mexico. Dr. Ann Barnett (2010, November) reports how she spent a year in Mexico doing neurological research at a hospital caring for severely malnourished children. She writes that most of the babies were so sick when they were admitted that they couldn't even cry.

Awareness is the birthplace of possibility. Everything you want to achieve begins here. As a new idea arises, it must gather power and influence. Other people must want to support it: the means to turn vision into reality must come to hand. All of these things depend on your awareness, because the moment you have a new idea, many paths lead to the future. At a deep place inside you, the right path calls out. The successful visionary looks inside, day after day, to find the next step in the path. (2010, Chopra)

One of the things we notice about America today, is that Americans often consciously and unconsciously promote leadership that is egocentric, overly market-and consumer-driven, and harmful or even violent to ourselves and others. It is an area in which we need both much help and deep healing in our nation. (2010, Ferch)

Throughout our walk we must not forget those who exhibit incredible passion, purpose, patience, and persistence. We find those who are painstakingly prepared, proactive, productive, and positive problem solvers. They far outweigh the numbers who demand our time and attention for unwise decisions.

"Let no one despise your youth, but be an example
to the believers in word, in conduct,
in love, in spirit, in faith, and in purity."
1 Timothy 4:12

Why Aren't You Telling Me?

Persuasion

Servant leaders rely on persuasion, rather than positional authority in making decisions. They seek to convince others, rather than coerce compliance. This particular element offers one of the clearest distinctions between the traditional authoritarian model and that of servant leadership. The servant leader is effective at building consensus within groups. Greenleaf (1996) wrote: "Persuasion involves arriving at a feeling of rightness about a belief or action through one's own intuitive sense."

Greenleaf was inspired in his work by John Woolman (1972). Woolman was an American Quaker who almost single-handedly rid the Quakers of holding slaves by 1770. Greenleaf noted: "Leaders work in wondrous ways. Some assume great institutional burdens; others quietly deal with one person at a time." Greenleaf continued by expanding on Woolman's servant leadership qualities: "His method was unique. He didn't raise a big storm about it or start a protest movement; his method was one of gentle but clear and persistent persuasion."

Vaclav Havel (2012), a passionate supporter of non-violent resistance, a role in which he has been compared to Mahatma Gandhi and Nelson Mandela. In the same manner as Gandhi and Mandela, Havel has been recognized for his outstanding contributions toward world peace and upholding human rights. In his quest for peace through persuasion rather than coercion, he stated: "The same word can be true at one moment and false the next, at one moment illuminating, at another, deceptive. On one occasion it can open up glorious horizons, on another, it can lay down the tracks to an entire archipelago of concentration camps. The same word can at one time be the cornerstone of peace, while at another, machine-gun fire resounds in its every syllable."

Persuasive communication is paramount to the servant leader. Communications' expert Thomas Gordon identified these "door slammers" or roadblocks to effective persuasive communication. These roadblocks to communication include but are not limited to: ordering, directing, commanding, admonishing, threatening, judging, criticizing, and shaming. These communication barriers are ineffective because they make a person feel ashamed, inadequate, resentful, guilty, defensive, and misunderstood.

Gandhi pleaded, "Go out to meet your antagonist in love, humility and openness, and you will change him."

The world will not find peace or be saved by combat, but by conference; not by bullets, but by brains; not by missiles, but by minds attuned to unconditional love and goodwill.

This humorous note speaks to the situation in which many of us sometimes find ourselves. "I connected my food processor to my computer in case I have to eat my words." It is important to be seen and heard in the field, and you need to work with your people on their turf. You can't manage by memo, and you can't sit behind your desk all day issuing orders or directions to your people. Max Depree (1989) summarized this well. He said, "Leadership is a serious meddling in other people's lives." The practice of managing by walking around is still applicable today.

Renowned psychologist William Glasser (1986), famous for his development of reality therapy and theories on choice and control, also believed in the importance of meddling in other people's lives. He noted that all people are born with five basic needs that motivate all their actions in life. By being aware of and appealing to these needs we can be more effective in our communication as leaders by responding to these needs. He identified these as survival, love, belonging, power, freedom, and love.

Persuasion begins with listening and connecting with people at their level. Maxwell (2010) says it very well in his book, "Everyone communicates, few connect." He states: "People need to know that you understand them. They need to sense that you're there for them. Good communicators understand that people do things for their own reasons, not for the reasons of the person doing the talking. Accordingly, they (good listeners) focus on their listeners' needs, not their own."

> "On life's journey, faith is nourishment, virtuous
> deeds are shelter, wisdom is the light by day and
> right mindfulness is the protection by night."
> Buddha

Why Do You Spend Your Time Dreaming?

Conceptualization

Servant leaders seek to nurture their abilities to "dream great dreams." The ability to look at a problem or an organization from a conceptualizing perspective means that one must think beyond day-to-day realities. Servant leaders must seek a delicate balance between conceptualization and day-to-day focus.

Sanders (2002) in his book, "Love is the killer app," shared a great acronym for the ingredients necessary for a successful business dream. D was for differentiation, R was for relevance, E was for esteem, A was for awareness, and M was for Mind's Eye. Differentiation is about being different in a positive, productive manner that can sustain itself over time. Relevance is determined to a large degree by the frequency with which something important appears in your life. Esteem is all about trust. Awareness is being recognized for your skills and talents. The promise you make and keep with your constituents is what is kept in their "Mind's Eye." (pp. 37-42)

Conceptualization builds a path into the future and communicates a profound message of commitment to all members of the organization. Taylor-Gillham (1998)

Conceptualization is a method of problem solving long before the problems themselves are manifested. It is about creating an explicit vision for the organization, modeling servant leadership qualities, and creating a unified effort of service to all constituents. Encouraging risk taking and creativity and creating opportunities for staff to come together to commit to collegiality are all part of the process of conceptualization.

Nothing happens until someone starts dreaming. If you don't have a goal, you have a goal by default. That goal is to do nothing. Aim at nothing and that is what you hit – nothing.

Whereas managers are maintenance thinkers; leaders by contrast are creative problem solvers. Leaders use their imagination to visualize new connections between ordinary events, to continually analyze and question the efficiency of the status quo, and to constantly ask the "what if" questions.

Mark Goldberg (2001) found that there were five large-minded qualities that effective leaders embrace. They are: 1) possessing a bedrock belief in the potency and usefulness of one's work; 2) having the courage to swim upstream, no matter how long it takes, and no matter what the obstacles, 3) being determined to exercise one's social conscience to make certain that everyone gets inside the tent; 4) maintaining a seriousness of purpose, which includes perseverance, integrity, and rigor; and 5) achieving situational mastery, the exact fit of one's individual talents to the task to be accomplished.

Unnecessary decisions not only waste time and resources, they also threaten to make all decisions ineffectual. Therefore, it is important that a leader be able to distinguish between necessary and unnecessary decisions.

Paul and Stroh in "Managing Your Time as a Leader" (2007) discussed the importance of managing time and its effect on decision-making. It involves working smarter, not harder. The assumption that working longer hours and more days in a year does not increase production. Rather, it causes increased stress and health problems, decreased effectiveness, and strained or failed relationships. The impact of overwork is sometimes clear and sometimes subtle – but it is dangerous, leading to a long-term decline in quality of life.

They pointed out that identifying and reducing the "phantom workload" will facilitate decision-making and increase productivity. They identified "phantom workload" as the work people unwittingly create for themselves by taking shortcuts around or trying to avoid essential, difficult tasks. As staff face the tasks they often avoid, they strengthen themselves to make hard decisions.

Finally, Paul and Stroh suggested managing time by mobilizing commitment, thinking strategically, building relationships and community, and organizing for action. All requests must be SMART requests: Specific, Measurable, Attainable, Realistic, and Time – Limited. If the request does not directly support the goals, it goes back to the originator for more information that meets the requirements of a SMART request.

In my own work, I wanted to help my middle management leaders with this challenge of knowing how to decide when to act and when to wait. I was frustrated when their first response to some problems was to overreact. So, I developed the matrix below to help them slow down and look carefully at the whole situation.

It was not intended to be a flowchart that forces an action but merely a list of choices that provides a mechanism to reflect before the leader reacts.

I entitled the matrix: "It's your choice."

It's your choice.		
Which is it? How do I decide?		
Problem	Dilemma	Catastrophe
Challenge	Predicament	Opportunity
Emergency	Crisis	Disaster
Difficulty	Trouble	Nuisance
Information		

Who does it belong to? Or Who needs to know?		
The goal is to choose as few as possible to accomplish what is needed.		
Only individual involved	Individual and guardian	Nobody
Grade level	Advisory	Spouse
All employees	Laborers	Specialists
Department	Business Office	Supervisor
Union	Confidant	
So…		
What do I do?		
Answer	Support	Deal with it
Avoid	Attack	Circumvent
Reply	Confront	React
Respond	Leave it alone	Wait and see
Listen	Enable	Smile
Gossip	Cry	Nothing

This is not rocket science, it is merely assessing every situation and determining the worth and necessity of the action. This involves serious reflection and foresight which we will hear about next. The leader considers the type or severity of the problem, then determines the person or people involved, and then decides upon an appropriate action. The keys are the questions: 1) Which is it? 2) Who does it belong to? And finally, 3) What do I do? Each of these questions helps the leader conceptualize and thus make the best decisions for all of those involved in the organization.

How Do You Know What's Going to Happen?

Foresight

"Surely mercy and goodness will follow
you all the days of your life"
Psalm 23:6

Greenleaf (1977) defined foresight as "a better than average guess about what is going to happen when in the future." This enables the servant leader to understand the lessons from the past, the realities of the present and the likely consequence of a decision for the future. It is deeply rooted in the intuitive mind. The foregoing decision matrix might as appropriately go with this lesson as in the lesson on conceptualization.

In leadership, the concept of now is a floating reality; now can mean almost "now" or "in the near future." We sometimes use the term "right now" to indicate "at this instant."

It's important to acknowledge that there is limited time available for any particular task or activity. It is artificial to assume that you can simply weight yourself or someone else down with work in the hopes that it will somehow get done. There are only a limited number of hours in the day and each hour spent working must be appropriately planned to generate the maximum possible output.

Foresight differs from conceptualization just as probabilities differ from possibilities. Developing foresight involves the gathering of information. Predictions and understanding of future possibilities must be based on an interpretation of the present and an understanding of the past.

Leaders rarely have every piece of information they need in order to make perfectly sound decisions. Yet if they wait for all pieces of information, the situation may change and they will have missed the opportunity. Therefore, leaders must be willing to take a risk with the information they have and move ahead.

By reviewing each item against the degree of urgency for the request, the position of the person making the request, the time it will take to complete it and the impact or consequence it will have; you have created the best possible set of screens for sorting the requests and putting them into the most appropriate order. This order gives the leader foresight and becomes the priority list numbered from the most important to the least important and then serves as the template for action.

Taylor-Gillham (1998) concluded that there are times when a leader must make a call or predict the pitfalls and threats related to an innovation with limited information. Sometimes a leader just has to go with his/her "gut feeling" or intuition. Intuition is a direct and immediate understanding, often manifested through sensory representation, but independent of apparent reasoning and without one's conscious attention. It's a "gut feeling." Foresight and intuition work together for the effective, visionary leader.

Elle Allison (2012) describes this type of leadership as being a resilient leader. After a setback, of which leaders have a multitude in which they encounter on almost a daily basis, a resilient leader does more than merely bounce back—they bounce forward. This is foresight and a lot more. With speed and elegance, resilient leaders take action that responds to new and ever-changing realities; even as they maintain the essential operations of the organizations they lead (Reeves & Allison, 2009, 2010). Good leaders lead with open eyes and courage to move forward.

Robert Schaffer (2010) in the Harvard Business Review identified four mistakes that leaders often make. I share these to reflect upon and self-examine so that foresight might rule before the mistake is made.

For the word executive, if it is more applicable substitute the word supervisor or leader.

First, managers fail to set proper expectations. When they announce major directional changes or new goals, they don't spell out credible plans or specify who's accountable. Second, they excuse subordinates from the pursuit of overall goals, allowing people to remain preoccupied with their own units. Third, executives essentially conspire with staff experts and consultants by going along with a deeply flawed product or process. Fourth, managers wait while associates over prepare. In other words, they don't get the job done in a timely fashion and the whole process is delayed. Perhaps, this goes back to the first mistake of not setting proper and clear expectations.

As I conclude this section I return to an example from the New Testament where we see throughout Jesus' life on earth, how he took time away for reflection, to call upon his Father to gain foresight such as that illustrated in the following passage.

> "Now it came to pass in those days that He went
> out to the mountain to pray, and He continued all
> night in prayer to God. And when it was day, He
> called His disciples to Himself; and from them He
> chose twelve whom He also named apostles."
> Luke 6:12-13

Why Do You Care about Those People?

Stewardship

In discussing stewardship, I am reminded of the traditional American folktale, "The Tale of Three Trees, Hunt (1989) shared the visions of grandeur three trees have for their lives. The first wished to become the most beautiful treasure chest in the world, the second wanted to be a strong sailing ship, and the third desired to be the tallest tree in the world. Fate turned their visions of grandeur to lives of service as the first tree became a manger for a baby, the second became a small fishing boat for frightened fishermen, and the third became the beams for a cross that would hold a man crucified for the sake of others. In a metaphorical sense, these three trees were transformed so they could demonstrate the kind of stewardship, sacrifice, and giving of oneself that is necessary to live a life of servant leadership.

Because you see, stewardship is not just about "giving." Quite a long time ago, Harvey Reeves Calkins (1915), a minister, wrote the book, "A Man and His Money." He wrote,

> "The generous man and the penurious man may err in equal measure, for the steward is not administering for himself, but for Another. Stewardship is the recognition that God is the owner of all economic value, and therefore, that private property can be no other than a

sacred trust. This then, is stewardship-that I recognize and acknowledge the lordship of Another. The powers and possibilities of my being are my Lord's estate. They are committed in honor to my care. They are therefore to be administered as a sacred trust. Every act of man's life is judged by this standard; every ambition becomes worthy or base as it keeps in mind this purpose."

And so, we might be able to one day hear these words: "Well done, my good and faithful servant."

Stewardship, as defined by Spears, is recognizing that servant leadership begins with the desire to change oneself. Spears (1995) noted, "Servant leadership, like stewardship, assumes first and foremost a commitment to serving the needs of others. Openness and persuasion in communication are emphasized rather than control." (p.5) Robert Greenleaf's view of all institutions was one in which CEO's, staff, directors, and trustees all play significant roles in holding their institutions in trust for the greater good of society.

Sergiovanni (1993) emphasized that leadership that counts is leadership that touches people differently. It involves emotions, values, and relationships. He wrote, "It is a morally based leadership—leadership that represents a form of stewardship, a commitment to serve others and to serve ideals" (p. 20). In a word, it is "authentic."

Henri Nouwen (1989) spoke similarly regarding ministers who are certainly expected to be servant leaders. He believed that a minister's service will not be perceived as authentic unless it comes from a heart wounded by the suffering about which he speaks...He said, "The great illusion of leadership is to think that others can be led out of the desert by someone who has never been there."

Morrie, in "Tuesdays with Morrie" admonished: "The way to get meaning into your life is to devote yourself to loving others, devote yourself to your community around you, and devote yourself to creating something that gives you purpose and meaning" (Album, 1997, p. 127).

What are the purposes of laws and court decisions that are intended to bring about equality and opportunity for those least served if these laws are not followed? My study of history is too limited to understand what the motivation was and often still is that causes us to single out groups of people as less worthy than others. Have we made significant progress since Plessy v. Ferguson in 1896? Although the law was made right with Brown v. Board of Education, we still do not treat all people the way they should be treated. I reference Plessy v. Ferguson here as a reminder.

> The sole dissenter in the Plessy v. Ferguson case was Justice John Marshall Harlan, who wrote: "The arbitrary separation of citizens based on race while they are on a public highway is a badge of servitude wholly inconsistent with the civil freedom and equality before the law established by the Constitution. It cannot be justified upon any legal grounds." Harlan defied the racist conventions of the day and stood on true Constitutional principles.

Thankfully the law has changed but has our behavior? I cringe as I observe the actions of our current national leader as he seems obsessed with destroying so much of all the democracy we had taken for granted.

In the more than 50 years since Brown vs. Board of Education, Kiel (2011, January) reports that relatively little has changed in the quality of the delivery of education in New Orleans. However, there is hope that it could occur now after it was mandated fifty years ago. "If reformers in New Orleans are able to focus on the goal of increasing access to quality educational opportunities, then the chance created out of the tragedy of Hurricane Katrina will not be wasted. It would be beautifully ironic if, thanks in part to a hurricane, the schools in the city whose segregated railcars gave us the Landmark Supreme Court Case Plessy v. Ferguson could finally deliver on that elusive promise of Brown v. Board of Education to equalize educational opportunities."

Juana Bordas, President of Mestiza Leadership International, shares this comment from her book, Salsa, Soul, and Spirit (2007); "African Americans had to come out of desegregation and the pain of racism and work hand in hand with communities that oppressed them. This could only happen through the important attributes of forgiveness, love, and reconciliation."

Much like Bordas and others who have been recognized in this book, Gregory Boyle (2011) has turned his thoughts into action as he has worked directly with gang members in the Los Angeles area. He emphasizes that, "Compassion isn't just about feeling the pain of others, it's about bringing them in toward yourself. If we love what God loves, then, in compassion, margins get erased. 'Be compassionate as God is compassionate,' means the dismantling of barriers that exclude."

Of course, New Orleans is just one example of what has not happened as a result of not serving the least of those in our society. Instead of mobilizing positive relationships, for the last fifty plus years, non-minority parents have moved out of the city to the suburbs, enrolled their children in private schools, or manipulated the system to have their children enrolled in the magnet schools that still failed to integrate the schools as the majority of the students in the magnet schools were white. Once again, I have to ask, why? What is this hang up we have with skin color? It shows us only the exterior. The good stuff is on the inside.

In the African American tradition, Sankofa means, "Return, go back, seek, and retrieve." Sankofa urges us to reflect on and learn from the past. Perhaps, there is hope that we might take the opportunity to learn from the past and make New Orleans an example for other communities aware of the importance of the attributes of forgiveness, love, and reconciliation.

Another example from the life of a person of color comes from an anonymous article (2011, January-Sojourners) about a young man who came with his family from Mexico in 1993 to New York. He was three years old at the time. For all practical purposes, he has been in the United States for the majority of his life. Speaking only Spanish when he arrived in the United States, he learned English very quickly and has excelled at every level of his schooling and has been recruited to many accelerated learning programs. Then at the age of twenty-one, he feared being deported as efforts to punish illegal aliens continues to escalate. He makes a poignant remark in his short diary of his life. During the church offering, he was asked to fill out an organ donor application. He writes: "I can't help thinking: If I died here in America, would my heart, lungs, and tissues be illegal, too? Wow! Words to ponder, for sure.

Don't ask me! You are the One who's in Charge!

Commitment to the Growth of Others

Greenleaf (1977) conceived that commitment begins with the absolute condition of liability for another and argued that all that is needed to rebuild community is for enough servant leaders to show the way by each demonstrating unlimited liability or commitment for a specific community-related group. He emphasized that servant leaders must love or be committed to the corporation if the corporation is to serve society better. That commitment is not directed to the corporation as an abstraction but to the people who are gathered to render the service for which the corporation is enfranchised. This attribute of commitment thus motivates the servant leader to focus on relationships with people thereby building up the group. In this way, the capacity of the group is enhanced.

So, how do I make decisions? Am I truly a participant or is our meeting time together just an opportunity for you to tell us what has already been decided? Sounds familiar, doesn't it? In so many cases, this is what happens. Rather than operating in this manner, decision-making in an organization ought to be a process in which the stakeholders have a voice that matters. Otherwise just tell me what's been decided and don't waste my time.

One of the more common group participation decision-making models is referred to as the "6 C's." The six elements are:

- ✍ **Construct** a clear picture of precisely what must be decided.
- ✍ **Compile** a list of requirements that must be met.
- ✍ **Collect** information on alternatives that meet the requirements.
- ✍ **Compare** alternatives that meet the requirements.
- ✍ **Consider** the "<u>what might go wrong</u>" factor with each alternative.
- ✍ **Commit** to a decision and follow through with it.

Of course, there are many other models depending on the purpose, the style and preference of the leader, and the group composition but this is one that is easy to remember and to follow so that all participants are aware of the process and can be involved in it.

Many of the elements of servant leadership that have been discussed up to this point foster a commitment to the growth of people. Servant leadership is an understanding and practice of leadership that places the good of those led over the self-interest of the leader. Servant leadership promotes the valuing and development of people; the building of community; the practice of authenticity; the providing of leadership for the good of those led; and the sharing of power and status for the common good of each individual, the total organization, and those served by the organization. Antoya Pantoya, in Bordas (2007), concludes:

> The whole purpose of leadership is to exercise one's power, knowledge, and access to change those aspects of society that are inequitable. The role of the leader is the role of advocacy—to change the oppressive and destructive situations in society.

Joseph (2006) in his dissertation on servant leadership identified service, empowerment, vision, love, humility, and trust as key attributes of the servant leader. In consideration of the commitment to the growth of people, empowerment is especially important as it involves effective listening, making people feel significant, and it promotes an emphasis on teamwork, valuing of love and equality.

Empowerment of others reduces the differential between individuals and thereby leads to collaborative approaches to communication and organizational performance. By leading with these attributes as well as the others mentioned throughout this text, servant leaders set service standards by their own behaviors. They lead by doing. They are actively engaged in helping, assisting, and meeting the needs of employees within the work setting. Therefore, they serve as models of service for all employees. Empowerment creates a reciprocal relationship between leaders and followers that demonstrates the fact that each one needs what the other has.

A commitment to the growth of others requires anthropomaximology. I love this word! I came upon it in a workshop I attended several years ago in which Bob Moawad presented, He was a very inspirational speaker who founded Edge Learning Institute. It is the study of peak performing individuals, teams, and organizations. Bob continued his many motivational workshops while he was battling cancer which he succumbed to in 2007.

 One of my favorite books on leadership: "Monday Morning Leadership" (2002) provides some advice on creating peak performance: The author, David Cottrell, calls it: "Filling Lots of Buckets." The leader does this by: 1) Knowing the main thing, 2) Giving feedback on performance, 3) Providing recognition, and 4) communicating the team score.

Paul's leadership and commitment to the growth of others is a model that has been well defined throughout the New Testament. Leadership begins with the heart and Paul had a heart that was consistent, contrite, courageous, convictional, committed, and captivated. In Acts 20: 18-24, we see how Paul lived steadily while moving among his people; he acted humbly and willingly showed his weaknesses; he didn't shrink from doing the right thing: he communicated his convictions boldly, he was willing to die for his convictions, and he showed that a surrendered man doesn't have to survive (Maxwell, 2002).

We have all encountered "late bloomers" who if left without encouragement, patience, and commitment, our organization would have been denied their talents, and they would have been denied success.

Two men, both professors, both diagnosed with cancer offer advice on the commitment of growth of people. Randy Pausch, in "The Last Lecture" (2008), said:

> When you see yourself doing something badly and nobody's bothering to tell you anymore, that's a bad place to be. You may not want to hear it, but your critics are often the ones telling you they still love you and care about you, and want to make you better.

Clayton Christenson, Professor of Business Administration at Harvard Business School, offered this advice:

> Don't worry about the level of individual prominence you have achieved; worry about the individuals you have helped become better people. Think about the metric by which your life will be judged and make a resolution to live every day so that in the end, your life will be judged a success.
>
> Each of these men in their own way emphasized the need to look for the best in others and to be with them as they travel along their journey in life.

"And Jesus came and spoke to them, saying, 'All authority has been given to Me in heaven and on earth. Go therefore and make disciples of all the nations, baptizing them in the name of the Father and of the Son and of the Holy Spirit, teaching them to observe all things that I have commanded you; and lo, I am with you always, even to the end of the age.'"
Matthew 28:18-20

Why Don't You just Tell us What to Do?

Teamwork

Hesselbein (1996) wrote, "We need to remember that we can do little alone and yet much together" (p. 3). Maxwell (1999) stated much of the same feeling in a slightly different way. He said, "One is too small of a number to produce greatness...We need to group up to grow up" (p. 28).

Effective leaders must work to build a cohesive community. Linda Wing (2005) suggested the following practices that are necessary for effective leadership in high-performance teams:

- Model the behavior you wish to see in others.
- Establish the vision and mission of the team.
- Speak in the language of the team with whom you are working.
- "Get out of the way" and allow team members to perform at their highest and most proficient levels.
- Building the infrastructure to accomplish your goals and assign individuals to the tasks where they can be most successful is critical.
- Inform team members how they can best put their knowledge and skills to work in the organization.
- Focus on the most relevant initiatives that have been identified as most critical to the organization.

- Support your team and give them confidence in your support.
- Get to know and understand the individual and collective needs of your team members. Understanding the needs for involvement, contribution, and overall social interaction of the team is of critical importance.

According to Spears (1995), the servant leader seeks to identify some means for building teamwork among those who work in a given institution (p. 6).

Work teams perform most effectively in a setting that is led by a transformational style of leadership such as we have been describing as servant leadership. It cannot be over-emphasized; servant leaders inspire and motivate others to exceed performance expectations. It is characterized by participation, information sharing, teamwork, vision, and enhancing the self-worth of others, which has significant effects on team motivation,commitment to the organization and trust in their leaders.

Organizations are increasingly searching for leaders who can exhibit these leadership qualities because organizations have become less stable and predictable, and strong bonds of trust are likely to be replacing bureaucratic rules in defining expectations and relationships (Robbins & Judge, 2007, p. 457-458).

It is necessary in the team building process that members learn how to manage conflict, how to evaluate performance of the group, and provide feedback and support that will encourage each member to meet their commitment to the team and the organization.

Among the characteristics which are critical in assessing the effectiveness of the team and creating trust among team members are the following: (Mealiea and Baltazar 2005, p. 9-10)

- Clear purpose where shared goals act to spark group effort by providing clear direction and buy-in.
- Consensus decision-making where all members are allowed to openly express their opinions and preferences.

- Shared leadership in the areas of collaboration, facilitation, challenging, and controlling the group processes.
- Very active listening that demonstrates an openness to achieve interpersonal understanding and sensitivity.
- Open communication where group members openly share their feelings and provide timely and relevant feedback.
- Self-assessment to assess and review performance, environments, and goals.
- Civilized disagreements to deal with the wide variety of conflicts that may occur within the group.
- Style diversity, when members actively seek out other members who may have differences that enhance the ability for the group to perform and develop.
- Networking to draw upon information, support, and assistance from others who are external to the group to facilitate maximum performance.

Without the observance of these essential servant leadership practices, trust will not be developed within the team.

Patrick Lencioni (2002) believes, "Teams that lack trust are incapable of engaging in unfiltered and passionate debate of ideas." When teams resort to veiled discussions and guarded comments it creates an artificial sense of harmony. If a team utilizes the characteristics suggested by Mealiea and Baltazar (2005), it is more likely they will function effectively and be able to cultivate the qualities of trust, healthy conflict, commitment, accountability, and a focus on collective results.

Heifitz and Linsky (2002) offer:

> "To lead is to live dangerously because when leadership counts, when you lead people through difficult changes, you challenge what people hold dear: their daily habits, tools, loyalties, and ways of thinking—with nothing more to offer perhaps than a possibility."

In an example from one of our Native American leaders, we see a display of servant leadership qualities. Chief Sitting Bull in "The Battle of the Big Horn" in 1876 encapsulates the leadership qualities of teamwork. Sitting Bull led through commitment, through service to others, He fused his destiny with that of his people. He gathered information from all levels of his people: other chiefs, scouts, tribe members, elderly, women, children, etc. He was in touch with all locations of the "Sioux" world. "Sitting Bull knew that he must first seek to understand his people before he could expect to be understood by them." (p. 74) He lived among his people, claiming no special privileges. He ate what they ate, slept where they slept, traveled among them, and shared the responsibilities of daily life. (Murphy, E. C., & Snell, M. (1993). " The Genius of Sitting Bull")

Heifitz also offers this great advice for leaders. I love the analogy of the dance floor because like leadership in an organization, there is so much happening all at once. His point is that leadership is kind of like a dance floor and there's a lot of things happening around you so sometimes you have to go up to the balcony and look at the whole dance floor and sometimes you need to mingle about with the dancers on the dance floor. You can't just hang out in one place and assume that all is going well.

It must be obvious by now that we all need each other to be successful. Warren Bennis (2000), one of the most respected leadership gurus of our time concurred. He held that current organizations are evolving into federations, networks, clusters, cross-functional teams, temporary systems, ad hoc forces, lattices, modules, matrices – almost anything but pyramids with their obsolete top-down leadership. The number of leadership roles one might play on a team is too numerous to mention but for an effective organization, there are surely to be such roles as an organizer to provide structure, a creator to initiate ideas, a promoter to champion the ideas, a maintainer to provide balance between groups, an advisor to find more information, a producer to provide direction and follow-through, an assessor to provide insight and analysis, and a controller to keep track of details. They might be called by different names and have slightly different descriptions, but these are the players that are needed on any effective work team.

Nelson Mandela is a leader who exemplified what James says is required for leadership. I am inspired by the persistence he shared in these words:

> I have discovered the secret that after climbing a great hill, one only finds more hills to climb. I have taken a moment here to rest, to steal a view of the glorious vista that surrounds me, to look back at the distance I have come. But I can only rest for a moment, for with freedom comes responsibilities. And I dare not linger, for my long walk is not yet ended.

This man has truly shown by his good life what wisdom comes from deeds done in humility.

"Who is wise and understanding among you?
Let him show it by his good life, by deeds done
in the humility that comes from wisdom."
James 3:13

Aren't we all Part of One Great Body?

Other Applications of Servant Leadership

Servant leadership is becoming a proven practice and is being applied in many different areas. A number of businesses have learned of the benefits of practicing servant leadership principles and realizing that we are all part of one great body. For example, TD Industries, Inc., a construction company, has been practicing the principles of servant leadership for more than thirty years. This company considers it essential that employees trust management to listen to and hear their thoughts and ideas. This company eagerly encourages the active participation of all of it's employees in improving processes that will better serve their customers (Lowe, 1996, pp. 46-47).

In another example, Ken Melrose (1996), CEO of The Toro Company wrote: "The Master of Men fittingly expressed the ideal of leadership when he said, 'Whoever wants to be great among you must by your servant.' These few words stand up against all the management books on the shelves today: the great leader is a great servant" (p. 20).

Herman Miller, Inc., a furniture company (Depree, 1989) has been regularly included among the top twenty-five firms on Fortune's list of the most admired companies in the United States. Max Depree, chair of the board of directors, stated: "When we think about leaders and the variety of gifts people bring to corporations and institutions, we see that the art of leadership lies in polishing and liberating and enabling those gifts" (p. 10). Depree added, "Leadership is more tribal than scientific, more a weaving of relationships than an amassing of information." (p. 3).

Dave Thomas, founder of Wendy's, asserted that certain ingredients are necessary for leaders to achieve success. He identified these attributes as honesty, faith, discipline, caring, teamwork, support, motivation, creativity, responsibility, courage, and generosity.

When the First Edition of this book was written, according to Fortune magazine's "100 Best Companies to Work For" elements that would be lauded as servant leadership principles are also common to these top companies: Synovus Financial Corporation, ServiceMaster Company, the Men's Wearhouse, and Southwest Airlines. The companies that make the list change each year, but the point is these companies reflect a high level of mutual respect, trust, pride, and camaraderie between and among management and peers. These companies offer extensive training and development and a philosophy that employment is for keeps.

The following diagram shows the relationship between a Healthy Organization and Servant Leadership.

Management Consultant Rob Lebow of Heroic Environments, Inc. described companies that work. They are companies where honesty is expected, where people are treated with trust and respect, and their contributions are acknowledged. They foster a climate of integrity on the part of managers and employees alike, and a climate that is conducive to risk-taking and new ideas. There must be a fitting balance of "tension" in a company. Having a company where everyone gives credit where credit is due, everyone tells the truth all of the time to everybody, and everyone is in the business of acting as a mentor to their underlings sounds like a corporate Utopia. However, it makes economic sense. They have found that the lower the amount of tension, the higher the amount of profitability.

Former Indianapolis Colts' Coach Tony Dungy is using his experiences to tell others about the importance of using your leadership skills for mentoring others. From his book, "The Mentor Leader," (2010) he states: "Mentor leadership focuses on building people up, building significance into their lives and building leaders for the next generation."

When networks of people are working toward the same end, it inspires much higher levels of creativity and self-expression. When they are subject to management by shared values, aspirations, and open boundaries instead of management by traditional controls, their energies and passions are engaged. Melrose (1996) concluded: The new wave of companies must capitalize on the creativity of each individual and promote a sense of community both inside and outside the office.

The companies that fit this description rely in part on clear standards and disciplines, including at the most basic level, standardized processes. Kanter (2008) in "Transforming Giants," indicated these companies draw heavily on their shared understanding of mission and values and provide a broad sharing of tools and information. Common values and standards help companies who share a diverse work force and are geographically disparate to make consistent and timely decisions.

Many companies and a variety of other organizations have followed the lead of the vendors at the Pike Place Fish Market in Seattle. They believe it is about finding ways to have more fun accomplishing serious goals. They have instituted four steps they call the "FISH Philosophy (1998)." The four steps include: 1) Be there, 2) Play, 3) Make their day, and 4) Choose your attitude. Number 1 is being fully present for one another. It is a great way to practice wholeheartedness and a way to fight burnout. Number 2 is about having fun. Number 3 speaks to practicing small, random acts of kindness. Few things are as rewarding and infectious as lifting another person's spirit. Finally, every person has the ability to choose their own attitude. You can look for the best or you can look for the worst. And it is a sure thing you will get that to which you focus your attention. It is a conscious choice that each of us has.

Sirota (2001) speaks to this same sense of sharing the burden and sharing the workload in a supportive, enjoyable environment. He affirms that:

> Most human beings have an enormous need to contribute, to take pride in their contribution, and to be proud of the organization in which they work. Companies suffer large hidden costs when they do not harness that energy.

Other examples of those who are reaching out to help the least privileged in society are Bono, the lead singer in the rock band U2. He has traveled throughout the world most notably on behalf of the fight to prevent and cure AIDS.

Peter Buffett (2010) is another one of our contemporaries who is an Emmy Award-winning composer, a New York Times best-selling author and noted advocate for social change. He is the leading voice of Change Our Story, a forum for conversation that encourages people to take an active role in shaping our future as a global community. This quote from Peter speaks volumes about social justice throughout the world: "How can we possibly follow the Golden Rule when the people who have the gold make the rules?"

Another example is Tony Blair, former Prime Minister of the United Kingdom from 1997 till 2007. Blair has supported a number of charitable causes with his most notable being the Tony Blair Faith Foundation.

This foundation provides leaders with the knowledge to understand the complexities of religion in the world. The foundation empowers young people with the knowledge and skills to understand the wide variety of religions, while opening their minds to respect and not fear differences. Moreover, the Tony Blair Faith Foundation provides the practical support required to help prevent religious prejudice, conflict and extremism.

These three gentlemen offer examples of how God is using people to help bring wholeness where there is division. God did say, all men and women not just some are created in His likeness.

Is there One Type of Person who Personifies a Servant Leader?

———————

The Myers-Briggs Type Indicator identifies sixteen different personality types. Everyone has one dominant function that may be intuition, sensing, feeling or thinking. Each person also expresses their dominant function primarily as an introvert or an extrovert. Finally, each person can be either judging or perceiving. However, as mentioned earlier the purpose of finding one or another's type is not to decide which is best but to recognize the strengths of each and learn to accept each person with the strengths and characteristics they present.

This is not unlike the model that Jesus gave us in selecting his disciples. He brought together a very diverse group of twelve men. There was a threefold purpose behind the call of the twelve: 1) that they might be with Him; 2) that He might send them out to preach: and 3) that they might have the power to heal sicknesses and to cast out demons. By being with Him first, there was a time of intimate training and preparation before they were sent out and to preach in public.

It is quite certain that the original group of twelve disciples was a group of young men most likely in their twenties. There was nothing wonderfully significant about the men themselves: it was their connection with Jesus that made them great. They were men of different backgrounds, temperaments and habits. They came together under the same roof to learn and to obey.

They were by name: Andrew, James, the son of Alphaeus, James, the son of Zebedee, John, also a son of Zebedee, Judas Iscariot, Matthew, Matthias, chosen to replace Judas, Nathanael, also called Bartholomew, Peter, also called Simon and Cephas, Philip, Simon the Canaanite and Zealot, Thaddaeus, and Thomas. (Mark 3:13-19 and Luke 6:12-16) (MacDonald, 1995)

These disciples were God-fearing people. Only this God-fearing characteristic bounded them to Jesus. Their integrity, justice and mercy cannot be denied. They were diligent, honest and pious people, and above all dedicated to the Lord and to His command. They were not men of high education, but neither were they illiterate. Most of them spoke Aramaic and Greek. They were educated in the knowledge of. God in Jewish synagogues, and they managed a discipline of high standards. Four of them were fishermen, one was a collector of taxes, and the rest belonged to the general working classes. (Life Application Study Bible, 1995) One might wonder if including women in this group might have enriched the group and added a rich dynamic to the work of these disciples. The presence of women may have given the women of the world some strong examples of discipleship to follow. Of course, there were women who followed Jesus closely, but they were not named in this select group who were specially chosen as leaders.

Jesus' conception of a human's worth, his emphasis on the sacredness and dignity of each individual has left its impact heavily on Western civilization. Jesus made it clear that humans are more than an amazing collection of chemicals — more than a bundle of drives, desires, urges, abilities and disabilities. He shares with these new followers these very basic instructions.

> "Brothers, think of what you were when you were called. Not many of you were wise by human standards; not many were influential; not many were of noble birth. But God chose the foolish things of the world to shame the wise; God chose the weak things of the world to shame the strong. He chose the lowly things of this world and the despised things—and the things that

are not—to nullify the things that are, so that no one may boast before him. It is because of him that you are in Christ Jesus, who has become for us wisdom from God—that is, our righteousness, holiness and redemption. Therefore, as it is written: "Let him who boasts boast in the Lord."

1 Corinthians 1:26-31

Jesus' comparisons-As the one who came not to be served but to serve, Jesus provided the pattern and the measure of his own ideal of servant leadership. (2006, October 16-America) Daniel J. Harrington

From my readings, these are some of the qualities I find in scripture:

Servant not rule-maker-Matt 20:26
Example not enforcer-1 John 2:6, John 13
Service to not power over-John 13: 14-15
Give not take-2 Co 8:7-9
Include not exclude-Romans 2:11
Forgive not blame-Col 3:13
Gestalt not segment-Luke 6: 27-28
Share not hoard-1 John 3:17, Acts 4:32-37
Complement not criticize-Rom 15: 2-3
Consensus not coercion-Phil 2: 2-4
Collectivism not individualism-Romans 12:8

Would we not gain far more as individuals and as communities if we took this knowledge of some of what we have read and heard from scripture and applied it to our own daily lives? I know I could certainly benefit. In addition to not showing favoritism and emphasizing forgiveness, we know that Jesus prayed-sometimes all night long while others slept. In John 17, He prayed for all of us and in Luke 14, He even gave us an example of how to pray. We know that He was tempted just like we are; that He explained and taught God's word in ways that most people could understand and He served others even to the extent of washing His disciples' feet. He also shared meals with His disciples and others and worked side-by-side with them giving them courage and inspiration. He embraced outcasts and healed the sick of mind, body, and spirit. He taught that visiting prisoners was equal to visiting God's anointed. He treated lepers, prostitutes, and people with mental illness with respect and healed the sick regardless of their legal status. He recognized the value of women and children in the same manner as He did all others. He challenged those who used religion to defend their manmade rules and traditions and taught leadership skills to others to ensure that what He taught would be sustained and carried on with integrity. The final and most important proof of his love for each of us was His suffering and dying on the cross and His resurrection from the dead.

Therefore, just as Jesus took His twelve and those that followed after, we as leaders must do the same with our followers. People need to have work where they can make full use of their gifts and talents so they can feel proud of what they accomplish. They want to have a say in the decisions that affect their work, and they want to see that there are actual opportunities for advancement and learning. When leaders fail to recognize these needs, followers become less than followers and they develop discontentment and begin to become leaders themselves of the other disgruntled workers. All people have genuine needs for meaning, purpose, connection, and inclusion in their life's work. Leaders cannot expect their people to leave their needs at the door while expecting them to passionately engage in their work. If these needs are not dealt with directly and respectfully, it will eventually be necessary to deal with the workers' negative behavior, discontent, and disengagement.

In most work situations in which I am familiar, leaders must play the hand they are dealt. It is not always as easy as Jim Collins (2001) says to get all of the people on the right seats on the bus. Even when it is possible, an effective leader must consider not only the needs discussed above but also the diversity of the employees. We must respectfully consider the diversity of ages, ethnicity, learning styles, temperament, and gender.

Just considering age, we have people working side by side who come from the industrial work ethic period of the 50's and early 60's who are described as practical and dedicated, the optimistic and driven baby boomers of the 60's and 70's, the skeptical and self-reliant Gen X workers of the 80's and 90's, the ambitious and hopeful from the Gen Y period, and most recently, the Gen Z folks born from 2001 to 2020. Now, we are starting with what is being referred to as Gen Alpha. The Gen Alpha group currently represents 48 million people in the United States. Alphas are being raised in homes with technology at their fingertips. Due to the pandemic many attended school virtually. We have yet to see how they will impact the future and how the future will impact them.

As we look at the diversity in all of our workers, We must also take a step back and look at ourselves. Sometimes when we think a problem is with others might it not be very possible that actually the problem is with us?

The person we think we are portraying or the qualities and sensitivities we are presenting may be far from what others are observing in us. As I have looked more closely at current research on the needs, desires, and strengths of each of the generational groups, it is an immense challenge to meet the needs of each individually and then take these differences and form them into an effective workgroup. The work ethic and expectations I have as a "Baby Boomer" are considerably different from the emerging workforce of those from Gen Y and beyond.

So, as I look at this multitude of needs, the idealist in me suggests how wonderful it would be if all of our relationships were responded to in a spirit of harmonious interest in one another's welfare. Our task as leaders is to orchestrate this harmony by considering and working with the multitude of individual gifts, talents, skills, and needs that our employees bring with them to work. This is a daunting task as our workplaces are transforming so fast that we cannot even envision what the future will hold. I have six young granddaughters and two grandsons. During the 50's, our parents had a vague idea of some of the occupations they dreamed that we might hold. Now we realize that the occupations my grandchildren will hold have not even been created. Their schooling has already changed drastically in the past few years. They are adjusting well but it is more difficult for us. With all that is available and developing in the world of technology, there may not even be the necessity to go outside our home for more education. Traditional school buildings may very well become a thing of the past as might also be true of traditional office buildings.

What we do know is that the type of effective servant leadership that Jesus modeled with His diverse group of disciples will continue to stand the test of time.

Numerous religious leaders have displayed these same servant leadership qualities. These leaders include but are not limited to: Mother Teresa, Mahatma Gandhi, Dr. Martin Luther King, Jr., Cardinal Joseph Bernardin of Chicago, Albert Schweitzer, Archbishops Raymond Hunthausen and Thomas Murphy of Seattle, Archbishop Desmond Tutu of South Africa, Pope John XXIII, Pope John Paul II, Pope Francis, Reverend Billy Graham, and many, many others. More currently, we have folks such as Simon Sinek, Patrick Lencioni, Brene Brown and Kim Savage, Executive Director for Hope International based in New Westminster, BC. and Cheryl Bachelder, former CEO of Popeye's Louisiana Kitchen. Note the diversity of fields of interest in the people named above which is testament that any of us can employ the qualities of servant leadership to improve our workplace and our world.

Each person who reads this text has their own examples from their own experiences and communities to include in this section and each of the others.

Mother Teresa, Dr. King, and Archbishop Tutu were Nobel Prize Winners. Smith (1964), in describing Gandhi's influence wrote, "Gandhi's message is simple, direct, and inescapable. Give what you have to the service of man—wealth, talents, energy, love—and receive it back in God's hands" (p. 309). As an admirer of Gandhi and Martin Luther King, Jr., Smith found they always looked to the needs of their followers. They sought justice, peace, and righteousness for all mankind.

After Chicago Cardinal Bernardin's death, Kloehn (1996) reported the following in the Chicago Times: "Where Bernardin wielded his influence, it was not always through edict—as it was for the bishops who ruled like kings in ages past—but through compromise, persuasion, and organizational ability" (p. 1). These attributes definitely illustrate the ways of the servant leader.

Closer to my home were former Archbishops Raymond Hunthausen and Thomas Murphy of Seattle. Servant leadership qualities that these men led with included the characteristics of wisdom, understanding, patience, courage, and compassion, which the Roman Catholic Church identifies as the gifts of the Holy Spirit (Scripko, 1992, p. 145). They were willing to take risks to serve and follow their beliefs even when their actions didn't completely align with the doctrine of their particular denomination, but their actions did align with what Jesus provided as examples.

Like these men, Pope John XXIII (1958-1963) who made a magnificent impression not only on the church but the whole world in a very short time is credited with this quote:

> "Consult not your fears but your hopes and your dreams. Think not about your frustrations, but about your unfulfilled potential. Concern yourself not with what you tried and failed in, but with what is still possible for you to do."

In like manner, Pope John Paul II (1978-2005) said, "Radical changes in world politics leave America with a heightened responsibility to be, for the world, an example of a genuinely free, democratic, just and humane society." This challenge becomes even greater when we realize that often our own churches put more emphasis on religious doctrine with all the man-made rules and mandates rather than on the Christian love and forgiveness that Jesus bought us with His suffering, death, and resurrection. Even our political parties do their best to create division rather than unity by suggesting that one party is more righteous than the other. Representative Joe Kennedy in a speech in 2017 to faith leaders, regarding our hateful divisions in our political parties:

> Ladies and gentlemen, this is the greatest threat we face.
> A rebuke of our highest American ideal—as old as the

scriptures and as clear as the Constitution. The belief that we are all worthy, we are all equal, we all count. In the eyes of our law and our leaders, our God, and our government. "Rich and poor have a common bond. The Lord is maker of them all."

Pastors and radio hosts openly criticize and chastise those who don't share what they interpret as right. We are even convinced by some of these zealots that it is a Christian virtue to sacrifice our own sons and daughters to kill our brothers and sisters in lands that don't believe exactly as we do. Until we embrace the power of the love of Jesus and His forgiveness, we cannot be free to serve others and share His love. We must be willing to accept ourselves and others not as we are at a specific moment but as God intended us to be.

Greenleaf (1977) referred to another religious leader who has been mentioned previously. John Woolman, an 18th century Quaker almost single-handedly rid the Quakers of slaves. His method was one of gentle, but clear and persistent persuasion. Throughout thirty years of his adult life, he traveled to fellow Quakers and one by one convinced them to abandon the practice of slavery. Significantly, this occurred almost 100 years before the Civil War (p. 29).

Another example of a religious application of servant leadership began with a trip to Mexico in 1982. The conditions encountered caused those present to ask many questions about the causes of poverty and racism as well as what role the Church should play as ambassador for reconciliation and transformation in today's fractured world. What began in a church basement with two volunteers in 1986 now draws others together to flesh out the mission of the Center for Sharing which is calling forth the gifts of all people through Christ-centered community.

Although the Center for Sharing had been informally raising up servant leaders and building programs around them since 1986, the first formal Servant Leadership course was held in 1995. Since 1995 local leadership formation courses have been held in Walla Walla, Pasco, Spokane, and Seattle Washington, Portland and Salem Oregon, San Diego California, Tijuana, Mexicali, and Juchitán Mexico, Nairobi and

Malindi Kenya, and in the fall of 2007 Kisumu Kenya and the spring of 2008 the Mindoro Bible College in the Philippines. Cheryl Broetje and Glenn Cross are the co-directors of The Center for Sharing where they are headquartered in Pasco, Washington. It began small but continues to grow immensely.

This is what Nelson Mandela meant when he said, "Your playing small doesn't serve the world. There's nothing enlightened about shrinking so that other people won't feel insecure around you. We were born to make manifest the glory of God that is within us. It's not just in some of us; it's in everyone."

During a period of time in my own life when I felt like my world was falling apart I was especially drawn to the words of Hebrews 10: 32-39 as I listened over and over to a taped sermon from a radio show by Charles Swindoll in which he preached on not giving up even when you feel you cannot sustain anymore. These words of encouragement to persevere in the midst of suffering still provide food for me to this day:

> "Remember those earlier days after you had received the light, when you stood your ground in a great contest in the face of suffering. Sometimes you were publicly exposed to insult and persecution; at other times you stood side by side with those who were so treated. You sympathized with those in prison and joyfully accepted the confiscation of your property, because you knew that you yourselves had better and lasting possessions. So do not throw away your confidence; it will be richly rewarded. You need to persevere so that when you have done the will of God, you will receive what he has promised. For in just a very little while, He who is coming will come and will not delay. But my righteous one will live by faith. And if he shrinks back, I will not be pleased with him. But we are not of those who shrink back and are destroyed, but of those who believe and are saved."
>
> Hebrews 10:32-39

With the number of poor and unemployed people in our nation and in the world, we must follow this example in Acts. We must also remember that poor and hunger don't always mean physically. There are so many who are poor in spirit and hungry for affirmation, belonging, and competence.

> "In everything I did, I showed you that by
> this kind of hard work we must help the weak,
> remembering the words the Lord Jesus Himself
> said, 'It is more blessed to give than to receive.'"
> Acts 20:35

Institutional and Public Sector Applications

Among institutional applications, the Centennial Medical Center is one example of servant leadership in action. Bill Arnold (1993), president of Centennial Medical Center in Nashville, Tennessee, embraces a style of leadership that he calls person-centered leadership. Person-centered leadership follows many of the same tenets as servant leadership. Person-centered leadership connects a staff member's self-esteem and personal goals to the vision and goals of the organization. Mr. Arnold's philosophy of treating employees adheres to these statements: "When you're in the presence of someone who has great passion for a chosen line of work and the intelligence and commitment to bring vision to reality in that field, you just know it. These people broadcast all the right signals and the message is very clear." (p. 89)

Centennial Medical Center's person-centered leadership has been successful because it was a marriage of a system's approach to quality improvement with a twenty-first century focus on each individual staff member's needs, strengths, and possibilities. In appearance, the most radical change Arnold made at Centennial was to literally take his office door off of its hinges. This symbolism and action was to let co-workers know that he, the president, was sincere about listening and being open to their spontaneous ideas and needs. This approach to leadership has not only improved the human climate of the institution, but it has also dramatically improved the other related business results and profits as well.

Jimmy Carter is another great moral leader of our time who must be considered a servant leader. Former President Carter may or may not be recognized as one of the greatest presidents of our country, but he is recognized as one the world's greatest humanitarians. Carter has been instrumental in many efforts to help the poor, eradicate diseases in Third World countries, fight segregation, seek peace throughout the world, and to spread his faith and moral convictions.

His role as 39th President of the United States has certainly helped him promote these efforts. Through the Carter Center he and his wife Rosalynn have been able to fight disease, hunger, poverty, conflict, and oppression. Through Habitat for Humanity, they have attacked poverty and helped people gain independence and respect by cooperatively building homes. Since his presidency, Carter has led an adult Bible class at his hometown church in Plains, Georgia (Macdonald, 1996). Dan Ariel (1996), President Carter's pastor and friend said, "Like Moses, who had claim to royalty but identified himself with the anguish of the Hebrew slaves, Jimmy Carter has had the power of a king but still has the heart of a servant" (p. 1) What an amazing compliment! At 97 years of age at this writing, former President Carter continues to advocate for social justice and improving the lives of others throughout the world.

A few other presidents have practiced some of these same characteristics of servant leadership. Our first President, George Washington, long before becoming president copied by hand 110 Rules of Civility & Decent Behavior and Conversation. He had this completed by the age of sixteen. These rules may have been taken from a set of rules composed by French Jesuits in 1595 and therefore may have been part of a penmanship lesson assigned by a schoolmaster. Regardless, it is interesting to note that they all have a common focus of regard for other people rather than the narrow focus of our own self-interests. As I reflect on these, I see the servant leadership elements of listening, empathy, healing, persuasion, perception, and conceptualization. Just a few examples that are great lessons for today include:

- "When you must give advice or criticism, consider the timing, whether it should be given in public or private; the manner and above all be gentle."
- "Show not yourself glad at the misfortune of another though he were your enemy."
- "Play not the peacock, looking everywhere about you, to see if you be well decked, if your shoes fit well if your stockings sit neatly, and clothes."
- "A man ought not to value himself of his achievements, or rare qualities of wit; much less of his riches, virtue, or kindred."

Similarly, on the night before he died, Franklin D. Roosevelt was in his cottage at Warm Springs, Georgia writing a speech to be given at the organization of the United Nations (Bailey, 2002). The last words Roosevelt wrote were:

> We seek peace – enduring peace – We must cultivate the science of human relations – the ability of all peoples, of all kinds, to live together and work together in the same world of peace…As we go forward toward the greatest contribution that any generation of human beings can make to the world – the contribution of lasting peace – I ask you to keep up your faith.

Real peace comes when God is glorified; peace is sought among all human beings, and good will is our attitude toward all persons. God hath called us to peace (1 Corinthians 7:15).

Robert F. Kennedy in an address at the University of California at Berkeley on October 22, 1966, challenged each person to do his or her part in being a leader as each of us is called. He stated:

> Few will have the greatness to bend history itself, but each of us can work to change a small portion of events, and in the total of those acts will be written the history

of this generation. It is from numberless diverse acts of courage and belief that human history is shaped. Each time a person stands up for an ideal, or acts to improve the lot of others, or strikes out against injustice, he sends forth a tiny ripple of hope and crossing each other from a million different centers of energy and daring, those ripples build a current that can sweep down the mightiest walls of oppression and resistance.

As I read these words, I hope that we still will strive to meet and achieve this challenge. Kennedy goes on to say how tempting it is for the fortunate among us to follow the easy and familiar paths of personal ambition and success rather than to reach out and touch the lives of those who are not among the fortunate. I would submit that being less fortunate does not have only to do with material wealth and comfort but also the hunger for approval, belonging, and recognition. These are the areas we can touch as servant leaders in our places of work.

In a speech at Stanford University several decades after Kennedy spoke the words above, Jim Wallis (2004) told the graduates and their guests: "We can do it if we want to badly enough." He said,

> For the first time in history, we have the information, knowledge, technology, and resources to bring the worst of global poverty virtually to an end. What we don't have is the moral and political will to do so. And it is becoming clear that it will take a new moral energy to create that political will.

There are many examples of people around the world who are trying to create that political will. The "New Statesmen" (2006) magazine dedicated a portion of its May 22, 2006 publication on the "Top 50 Heroes of Our Time." They identified hero as a man or woman whose actions have been in the service of the greater good and whose influence is national or international; someone who is prepared to act in pursuit of a freer, more equitable and democratic future, with recourse to violence. Some of the qualities that were identified were honesty, social justice, uncompromising principles, moral courage, and foresight, a beacon of hope, idealistic and driven to make a difference and a voice for those whose voices are not heard.

Paul shares a very similar message with the Philippians, one day at a time, one foot in front of the other; each of us can make a difference.

> "Brothers and Sisters, I do not consider myself yet to
> have taken hold of it. But one thing I do: Forgetting
> what is behind and straining toward what is ahead,
> I press on toward the goal to win the prize for which
> God has called me heavenward in Christ Jesus."
> Philippians 3:13-14

Educational Applications

Although not abundantly obvious in traditional public school educational systems, there have been a few applications of servant leadership in the area of education. Actually, I would say that most people that serve in traditional public schools and other private schools exemplify the tenets of servant leadership each and every day. It is just that as a system, it has not been a primary focus. I am eager for the day when it will be a part of each mission statement.

However, Egan (1994), another student of servant leadership, wrote about two contemporaries of Greenleaf who embraced the philosophy of servant leadership. Both men did their work in the area of experiential education before Greenleaf began his writing on the topic of servant leadership.

In 1949, Alec Dickson developed a program for voluntary leaders in Africa. His programs spread to Iraq, Austria, and the United Kingdom, and inspired over 30,000 volunteers. Dickson founded two volunteer training organizations, Voluntary Service Overseas and Community Service Volunteers.

Another contemporary of Greenleaf, a former Nazi concentration camp prisoner, Kurt Hahn, started Outward Bound in 1941. Outward Bound Schools have been opened around the world to challenge youth and to develop in them a commitment to serving others through self-awareness. The example set by these servant leaders and others could be referred to as the "critical multiplication factor" which implies that those who set the example will impart their commitment to those nearest to them (Egan, 1994, pp 16-17).

In another educational application, students at Wright State University in Dayton, Ohio have designed and implemented a student leadership program based on the concepts of servant leadership. The two-year program attracts students who are interested in developing an unselfish leadership style characterized by commitment to others. Service is an essential component of the Wright State University's mission (Seitz & Pepitone, 1996). Taken from the most recent University webpage we find the statements supporting their leadership mission.

We transform the lives of our students and the communities we serve. We are committed to:

- achieving learning outcomes through innovative, high-quality programs for all students: undergraduate, graduate, and professional.
- conducting scholarly research and creative endeavors; and to
- engaging in significant community service.

   Wright State's pursuit of excellence as a public university requires that it achieves and maintains an intellectual, cultural, and social environment in which all members of the university community are free to learn. Each member has a potential contribution to make to the whole, and it is our duty to encourage and promote that contribution. Our daily life is enriched by the diversity of individuals, groups, and cultures. Our exposure to new ideas and to new ways of experiencing and understanding life helps us learn and appreciate the diversity of the world. It helps us to value and maintain an environment in which personal dignity and respect for the individual are recognized by all.

Walker (1997) in another case of servant leadership in an educational setting asserted that Crowder College, a community college in Neosha, Missouri, may have been the only college in the United States to incorporate the theory of servant leadership as a component of it organizational practice. Walker stated: "Servant leadership is a pivotal theory that addresses both the theoretical and ethical methods of community college leadership" (p. 5). This provides a valuable opportunity to strengthen the ability of the institution to better serve its student population. At the inception of the community colleges back in the 1940's, these schools demystified higher education for a group of students who may not have considered a college education. They also opened additional doors of educational opportunities for women and minorities. Similar to the servant leadership theme of the mission of Wright State University, Crowder College attempts to build a civil, serving, literate, learning community of responsible citizens through the development of the following values:

> As a college family, Crowder is continuously engaged in: Caring: in honoring the inherent worth of each individual
> The pursuit of learning: in putting into practice the best that is known about how people learn.
> Fostering creativity and innovation: in exploring new ideas, trying new approaches, encouraging calculated risks when the potential results merit risk.
> Ethical behavior: in demonstrating through personal action that people should relate to each other ethically.
> Collaboration: in ensuring that every person in the organization shares in shaping the college's future.
> Serving others: in helping each person become freer, wiser, and better able to serve.

Since Walker's study, many community colleges and universities throughout the United States have incorporated the theory of servant leadership into their colleges by offering special programs in servant leadership. They have dedicated administrative positions to servant leadership, and/or established departments to teach and spread the theories of servant leadership.

In a study of public-school superintendents, Wheaton (1999) found that staff participants in selected public schools identified effective superintendent leadership with characteristics which could be associated with the servant leadership elements of listening, empathy, foresight, awareness, conceptualization, and teamwork. The elements of persuasion, healing, reflection, and stewardship seemed to be either less important to these participants or less easy to identify.

One of the biggest challenges of being a school leader today is to balance the tension between standards and soul. A school based solely on standards could easily become an arid, numerical, test-driven landscape that cannot nourish a total learning experience. There is the danger of turning teachers into merely managers and students into robots. However, without sacrificing accountability, without undermining quality, school administrators can choose to cultivate their own leadership and those they lead with a host of practical strategies that allow them to genuinely nurture each other in the process of building school communities where learning can thrive and teaching can be a calling. (Kessler, 2002)

Elmore, in Graseck (2005) stated, the best teacher to administrator relationship is one where the leaders teach by treading lightly, not being too quick to assert their authority. They stand tall without feeling superior and without wearing a badge of hierarchy. They listen and are open to criticism without defensiveness. They exercise care in making and keeping promises and they demonstrate humility, honesty, trust, and integrity.

In yet another educational setting, we have those students and staff who have been recipients and/or exemplified servant leadership in the area of athletics. I would be remiss if at some place and at some point in this discussion of servant leadership, I didn't include those high-profile coaches who I believe are also educators and have gone outside of what is considered the norm for coaches and have exhibited many of the qualities of servant leadership. Names that immediately come to my mind are John Wooden, Tony Dungy and Coach K from Duke University.

John Wooden (2009) in his Pyramid of Success included the qualities of cooperation, loyalty, cooperation, alertness, team spirit, poise, and skill as essential leadership skills. He also advocated ingredients of leadership where the leader is not consumed with himself and is deeply and vitally concerned with those under his leadership. He advocated also that the leader make every effort to convince those under his supervision that they are working with him rather than for him in order to accomplish the given task.

Tony Dungy was another one of the exceptions. He was not known to be a yeller, and he did not lead or motivate with fear. Instead, he believed in putting the right personnel in place, building a winning strategy based on the strengths of that personnel, and then treating them with the respect they deserved as professionals and human beings. This strategy worked exceptionally well for him and his teams.

Even after the death of their eldest son, James, to suicide, Dungy was still convinced that all things work together for good for those who love the Lord. Dungy compared his leadership as a coach and as a father as very similar. Both of these vocations require a lot of listening and developing fruitful relationships.

Joe Gibbs (2003) was another such leader and coach. When Gibbs won his third Super Bowl in 1992 with the Washington Redskins, his place in NFL history was secured. At nearly the same time, he was launching a venture as manager of a NASCAR racing team. Although Gibbs did his best to follow the model of Christ's leadership, he never forced it on anyone or laid on any guilt or acted pious about his faith. He felt that when it came to faith, it was up to the individual to decide. His players and those he worked with confirmed this. One of them indicated there was just something about Gibbs as a person and as a leader that made people want to follow him. They were drawn to his example of moralism, faith, and humility.

Many other coaches throughout the years such as Dallas Cowboys' former coach Tom Landry (2009) that exemplified this same type of leadership were influenced by and were involved with the Fellowship of

Christian Athletes. This organization was formed in 1954 in Stillwater, Oklahoma. The purpose of the organization was to help athletes model the type of Christ like leadership on and off the field that is being advocated in this book. The FCA has affected athletes and coaches who have made their mark in all walks of life including medicine, law, education, the arts, and virtually every other discipline.

Now that we have had the opportunity to look at all of the elements of servant leadership, it is as apparent to me as it was to Taylor-Gillham (1998) who noted how difficult it is to separate the elements or the hats we wear to practice the art of servant leadership. It is almost as though you cannot have one without the others. She suggested that servant leadership is a process made up of interdependent, integrative practices. She stated, "Although each characteristic and principle can stand alone, it is the combination and complimentary events that construct the philosophy and principles of servant leadership."

Leadership is about wearing lots of hats and choosing
the right one for the right situation and choosing
the right one for the specific relationship.

Leadership for the Future

Conclusion

As fast as things are happening in our world, it is appropriate to say the future is now. Most of the leadership styles, theories, applications, and practices discussed before that are described as servant leadership or are similar to servant leadership are as appropriate for the future as they are now and as they have been since the time of Christ and before through our indigenous ancestors and those from other ancient faith traditions. Leadership is about relationships with one another – it starts with family members and spreads throughout the whole world to international business transactions and peace talks. There is an African term I have come upon in several readings. It is "ubuntu," which is summed up by the saying, "I am because we are." No person is an island or can be a success without help and expertise from others.

According to Hill (2008), "leadership is about making emotional connections to motivate and inspire people, and our effectiveness at doing this has strong cultural overtones." (p. 126) Leaders need to continue to adopt a more inclusive, collaborative style. It's also becoming clear that today's complex environment demands a team approach to problem solving. This requires a leader who is comfortable sharing power and is generous in doing so. She is able to see extraordinary potential in ordinary people and can make decisions with a balance of idealism and pragmatism.

She goes on to say, "Leadership is a collective activity in which different people at different times—depending on their strengths—come forward to move the group in the direction it needs to go." It is about developing the talents of members so that they too can flourish in their roles—so they themselves can be nurtured as leaders and grow and lead.

Power grows exponentially – People are empowered. "One person can have a profound effect on another. And two people...well, two people can work miracles. They can change a whole town. They can change the world." (Frolov and Schneider, Northern Exposure, Cicely, 1992)

Leadership for the future will require the power of faith, the yearning for life-long learning, balance, the qualities of integrity, passion, and the desire to achieve one's personal best. These leaders will value diversity, respect the past, be action-oriented, and possess superb communication skills. We have regressed considerably from when we had a president that from all history has taught us to try to incorporate all of the lessons of the past, his knowledge of the present, and his hope for the future as he served as our president. Hopefully, we will get back to and continue in those days of hope. It is going to take a while to recover from the divisiveness we are experiencing in the ensuing years. We must regain a sense of hope for a greater tomorrow for our children and our children's children.

Wallace and Trinka (2008) suggested that leadership for the future will not be as much about pay, power and control over others, nor the opportunity to bask in the limelight. Great leaders understand their own beliefs and why they lead. They let go of their desire to control people and organizations through positional power or the force of their personalities. They tear down these barriers; fight the power of conformity of highly structured organizational cultures. They develop deep relationships with those they serve, and their total commitment is in moving other people to commitment (p. xv). They care about how their employees are doing on the job and demonstrate their care with visibility.

Great leaders model both teaching and learning. They know that when they stop learning, they stop leading. They never consider that they have arrived but rather are always seeking new perspectives, investigating what makes others successful, and reflecting on how they are leading. The main mark of successful leaders is not so much their impact on the present but more on the number of good leaders they leave behind who can go even further.

Ella Cora Deloria, was one of those leaders who was born on the Yankton Indian Reservation in South Dakota in 1889 who helped preserve records of the Sioux people. Her work is still used to study Sioux culture, ethnography, and language. In a comparable way, Aritana Yawalapiti from Brazil has shared his leadership legacy by teaching about his tribe and promoting the issues that affect the preservation of land, cultural heritage, education, and access to health resources. (Yesica Balderrama (2021, October 10)

Womble (2005), speaking at a Leadership Conference in Toronto, Canada, confirmed what leadership is all about. She stated, "Your leadership legacy is the sum total of the difference you make in people's lives, directly and indirectly, formally and informally. What we say and do today and every day will determine our leadership legacy."

Sanders (2002) agreed. He said, "Success in the future will be based on the fuzzy intangibles; the way you speak as a leader, the culture you nurture, the processes for managing information you set up for your people, the partnerships you form around technology's opportunities and challenges. Put your efforts into your people and the fabric of your company."

Former longtime CEO of Hanover Insurance, Bill O'Brien (2008) spoke of the need to embrace similar key values that are at the heart of bringing about the best in its members and thereby creating a successful organization. These four key values of which none stand alone are localness, merit, openness, and leanness.

Very briefly, O'Brien defined them as follows:

1. Localness is the distribution of power so that decisions are made by those closest to the source of action.
2. Merit means being sure that all decisions are aligned with the goals and values of the organization.
3. Openness is the transparency of the flow of information throughout the organization.
4. Leanness is the responsible stewardship of the organization's resources so that its economic health is maintained in both good and bad times.

As we see once again, the terms are a little different, but the ideas are not in conflict or contrary with those expressed and supported throughout this book.

It is a life of constant and constructivist learning. Jesus showed us what it meant to have to crawl and He continues to show us this legacy through His word. Creating a legacy, developing deep relationships, offering total commitment, and teaching and learning is what Jesus showed us during His time on earth. In John 15, He says, "You should produce much fruit and show that you are my followers, which brings glory to my Father." He continues, "I loved you as the Father loved me. Now remain in my love." This fruitfulness is not expected of just some of us. Jesus expects each of His followers not only to bear fruit, but to bear much fruit. We can see from His choice of disciples. It depends not on our talents but on our relationship with our Lord and all of our brothers and sisters.

We can even hear the same message in the lyrics of country-western singer John Michael Montgomery's song, "Life's A Dance."

> Life's a dance, you learn as you go
> Sometimes you lead, sometimes you follow
> Don't worry about what you don't know
> Life's a dance you learn as you go

The longer I live the more I believe, you do have to give if you want to receive. There is a time to listen, a time to talk and you might have to crawl even after you walk.

As noted earlier in this section, the not-so-distant future will be vastly different from what we see today. The rapidly changing demographics which are not limited to diverse languages, races, gender preferences, family structures, and religious beliefs and values will all impact the way we live.

Communication in this new world will continue to be affected, better or worse, by advances in the transmission of data through the media and the internet and the sensitivity with which that data is transmitted.

For many of the more fortunate in the world, it will be commonplace for work and school to occur in places other than what we are accustomed to. By way of virtual resources, work, school, vacation, meetings, and other gatherings may all be integrated. Many are already taking advantage of this type of venue to control most areas of their lives. Websites, blogs, and social networking provide opportunities never before even imagined. The "Modern Servant Leader," developed by my friend, Ben Lichtenwalner, Linkedin and Facebook already provide limitless access to just about any kind of information one might need to find. Although we can't foresee the future, we do know that we will want our lives to be filled with contentment, connection, and purpose.

An area of great interest to me is education for the future. I am convinced it will look very different. From the time and place, the teaching and the learning, the students and personnel, and the governance of schools all have the potential for major changes. As fast is all of this is happening, how do we have the foresight to plan responsibly?

The Christian leader or any leader of the future for that matter, is the one who truly knows the heart of one's faith. For me, it is God as He has become flesh, "a heart of flesh" in Jesus. Knowing God's heart means consistently, radically, and very concretely to announce and reveal that God is love and only love, and that every time fear, isolation, or despair begins to invade the human soul, this is not something that comes from God (Nouwen, 1989). I'm sure this can be stated in similar ways by leaders of each of the major faiths and cultural traditions.

Chief Dan George (1899-1981), who was Tribal Chief of the Tell-tall-watt tribe of North Vancouver, Canada for twelve years, shared these important words that apply to all people everywhere.

> It is hard for me to understand a culture that not only hates and fights his brothers but even attacks Nature and abuses her. Man must love all creation, or he will love none of it. Love is something you and I must have. We must have it because our spirit feeds upon it. Without love, our self-esteem weakens. Without it our courage fails. Without love we can no longer look out confidently at the world. Instead, we turn inwardly and begin to feed upon our own personalities and little by little we destroy ourselves.

As we learned earlier from Ken Melrose: "The Master of Men fittingly expressed the ideal of leadership when He said, 'Whoever wants to be great among you must be your servant.' These few words stand up against all the management and leadership books on the shelves today. The great leader is a great servant."

As the reader can see from the number of references that follow, a book like this is merely an invitation to adopt the servant leadership style and continue to investigate ways to apply it. Each day, I read about or witness people from all walks of life who are doing their best to lift up and serve others. We really are all leaders because as Martin Luther King Jr. said, "you only need a heart full of grace, a soul generated by love and you can be that servant."

Bibliography

Akpan, V. (2021, January 19). Greatest & famous servant leaders: 57 best in the world's history. Suntrust Blog. https://suntrustblog.com/

Albom, M. (1997). Tuesdays with Morrie. New York: Doubleday.

Allison, E. (December 2011/January 2012). Vol. 69, No. 4. Educational Leadership, ASCD Alexandria, VA.

Anonymous. (2011, January). Armed with a burning patience. Sojourners. Washington, DC. www.sojo.net

Arial, D. (1996, July). A conversation with Jimmy Carter's pastor. [Online]: Available: Zondervan Press Syndicate.

Arnold, W., & Plas, J. M. (1993) The human touch. New York: John Wiley & Sons, Inc.

Bailey, A. P. (2002, December 24) Bread of life. Cooper's.

Banuelos, M. V. (2003). The test of servant leadership. weLEAD online magazine. Leadingtoday.org.

Barnett, A. (2010, November). All in the family. Sojourners. Washington,DC. www.sojo.net

Bass, B. M. (1990). Bass & Stogdill's handbook of leadership: Theory, research, and managerial applications. New York: The Free Press.

Bass, B. M. (1997). Improving organizational effectiveness through transformational leadership. Thousand Oaks, CA: Sage Publications.

Batten, J. (1998). Servant-leadership: A passion to serve. In Spears, Larry C., Insights on Leadership, Service, stewardship, spirit, and servant-leadership (pp. 38-53). New York: John Wiley & Sons, Inc.

Bennis, W. (2000). Managing the dream : Reflections on leadership and change. Cambridge, MA: Perseus Books Publishing, LLC.

Berquist, W.H. (1992). The four cultures of the academy. San Francisco, CA: Jossey-Bass Inc., Publishers.

Blair, T. Tony Blair Faith Foundation. London, UK: http://www.tonyblairfaithfoundation.org/page/contact-us

Blanchard, K. (1998). Servant-leadership revisited. In Spears, Larry C., Insights on leadership: service, stewardship, spirit, and servant-leadership (pp. 21-28). New York: John Wiley & Sons, Inc.

Block, P. (1993). Stewardship: Choosing service over self-interest. San Francisco, CA: Berrett-Koehler.

Bordas, J. (2007). Salsa, soul, and spirit. San Francisco, CA: Berrett-Koehler.

Boyle, G. (2011). Tattoos on the heart. New York, NY: Simon & Schuster.

Brunner, C. C. (1997, June). Exercising power: A study differentiates authoritarian and collaborative decision making among superintendents. The School Administrator, 54, (6), 7-12.

Bryant, J. H. (2009). Love leadership: A new way to lead in a fear-based world. San Francisco, CA: Jossey Bass.

Buffett, P. (2011). Life is what you make it: Find your own path to fulfillment. New York, NY: Three Rivers Press.

Burgess, G. J. (2010). Dare to wear your soul on the outside. San Francisco, CA: Jossey Bass.

Burns, J. M. (1978). Leadership. New York: Harper & Row.

Calkins, H.R. (1915). A man and his money. The Methodist Book Concern. New York: NY.

Cameron K. S. & Freeman, S. J. Cultural congruence, strength, and type: Relationships to effectiveness. Research in organizational change and development. Vol. 5, pp. 23-58.

Center for American Progress (2022). https://www.americanprogress.org/about-us/diversity-and-inclusion/

Chinn, P. (2012). Peace and power: new directions for building community. Burlington, MA: Jones and Bartlett Learning.

Chopra, D. (2010). The soul of leadership. New York: Crown Publishing Group.

Christensen, C., Allworth, J. & Dillon, K. (2012). How will you measure your life? New York, NY: Harper Business

Clinton, R. J. (1993). Leadership perspectives. Altadena, CA: Barnabas Publishers.

Collins, J. (2001). Good to great. New York, NY: Harper Collins.

Cottrell, D. (2002). Monday morning leadership. Dallas, TX: CornerStone Leadership Institute.

Covey, S. R. (1996, April). Line-of-sight leadership. Executive Excellence,13, (4), 5-6.

Cowley, J. (2006, May 22). The top 50 heroes of our time. New Statesmen, Volume 135, Issue 4793.

Crosbie, R. (2005). Learning the soft skills of leadership. Industrial and commercial training , vol. 37 , no. 1 , 2005, p. 45-51

Daft, R. L., & Lengel, R. H. (2000). Fusion leadership. San Francisco, CA: Berrett-Koehler Publishers, Inc.

Deal, T. E., & Kennedy, A. A. (1982). Corporate cultures: the rites and rituals of corporate life. Cambridge, MA: Perseus Books Publishing, LLC.

DePree, M. (1989). Leadership is an art. New York, NY: Dell Publishing.

Dreamer, O.M. (1999). The invitation. New York: NY: Harper Collins.

Drucker, P. F. (1993). Managing for the future: The 1990's and beyond. New York, NY: Penguin Books.

Dungy, T. (2010). The mentor leader. Carol Stream, ILL: Tyndale House Publishers.

Ebener, D.R. (2011, February). Servant leadership and a culture of stewardship. The Priest. Our Sunday Visitor, Inc.

Egan, T. (1994, August 1). Samaritan leadership. The journal of experiential education, 17, (2), 13-17.

Eisenhower, D.D. (1953, April 16) Speech to the American Society of Newspaper Editors. "The chance for peace."

Epps, J. (2003, No. 5, Spring). The journey of meaning at work. St. Paul, MN. Group Facilitation: A Research and Applications Journal: International Association of Facilitators.

Ervin, G. D. (1997). The Jesus style. Cathedral City, CA: Yashua, Publishing.

Eva, N., Robin, M., Sendjaya, S., van Dierendonck, D., & Liden, R.C. (2019). Servant leadership: A systematic review and call for future research: The Leadership Quarterly, 30, 111-132.

Fawcett, S.E., Brau, J.C, Rhoads, G.K., & Whitlark, D. (2008, March). Spirituality and organizational culture: Cultivating the abc's of an inspiring workplace. International Journal of Public Administration, 31, (4), 420-438.

Ferch, S. (2010). Servant leadership: a way of life.

FISH Philosophy,)2020). Fish!: A Proven Way to Boost Morale and Improve Results. Lundin, Stephen, C.

Foley, C. (2010, October). Hungry for the homily, fed by the word. Liguorian. Palm Coast, FL: Liguorian Press.

Fortune Magazine 100 best companies to work for. http://www.greatplacetowork.net/best-companies/north-america/united-states/fortunes-100-best-companies-to-work-forr

Frankl, V. (2006). A Man's Search for Meaning, Boston, MA: Beacon Press

Frolov, D. & Schneider, A. (1993) Northern Exposure, Cicely.

Fullan, M. (2003). The moral imperative of school leadership. Thousand Oaks, CA: Corwin Press.

Forester, J. (1989). Planning in the face of power. CA: University of California Press.

Gardner, J. W. (1990). On leadership. New York: The Free Press.

Gibbs, J. & Abraham, K. (2003). Racing to Win. Colorado Springs, CO: Multnomah Books.

Giuliani, R. (2002). Leadership. New York, NY: Hyperion.

Glasser, W. (1986). Control theory in the classroom. New York, NY: Harper & Row.

Goldberg, M. (2001). Lessons from exceptional school leaders. Alexandria, VA: Association for supervision and curriculum development.

Gordon, T. (2001). Leader Effectiveness Training: L.E.T. New York, NY: Perigee Trade.

Graham, B. (1999). Just as I am: The autobiography of Billy Graham. San Francisco, CA: Zondervan.

Graseck, P. (2005, January). Where's the ministry in administration? Attending to the souls of our schools. Phi Delta Kappan.

Greenleaf, R. K. (1977). Servant leadership: A journey into the nature of legitimate power and greatness. Mahwah, NJ: Paulist Press.

Greenleaf, R. K. (1977). The servant as leader. Peterborough, N. H.: Center for Applied Studies.

Greenleaf R.K. (1998). The power of servant leadership. San Francisco, CA: Berrett-Koehler Publishers.

Greenleaf, R. K. (1996). On becoming a servant leader. San Francisco, CA: Jossey-Bass Publishers.

Gulley, P. (1998). Home town tales. Sisters, OR: Multnomah Publishers.

Hadden, R. & Catlette, B. (2001). Contented cows give better milk: The plain truth about employee relations & your bottom line. Germantown, IN: Saltillo Press.

Haines, T. L, & Yaggy, L. W. (1882). The royal path of life. Kansas City: MO: Wever & Co.

Halfacre, J.D., (2011, January/February). It's the little things. Principal. National Association of Elementary School Principals.

Hallowell, D. (2011). Shine: Using brain science to get the best from your people. Harvard Business Review Press.

Harrington, D. (2006, October 16) America

Heifitz, R. A., & Linsky, M. (2002). Leadership on the line: Staying alive through the dangers of leading. Harvard Business School Press.

Heil, G., Stephens, D.C., & Bennis, W.G. (2000) Douglas McGregor, Revisited: Managing the human side of the enterprise. New York, NY: John Wiley & Sons, Inc.

Hesselbein, F. (1996). The leader of the future. San Francisco: Jossey-Bass Publishers.

Hill, L. A. (2008, January). Where will we find tomorrow's leaders? Harvard Business Review. Leadership strategy for the twenty-first century.

Hodgkinson, C. (1991). Educational leadership, A moral art. Albany, NY: State University of New York Press.

Holifield, M. (1993). The servant's attitude: An ethical code for administrators. Educational Planning, 9, (2), 35-41.

Hoy, W. & Miskel, C.G. (2013). Educational Administration: Theory, research, and practice. New York, NY: McGraw-Hill Companies.

Hunt, A. E. (1991). The tale of three trees: A traditional folktale. Oxford, England: Lion Publishing.

Jaworski, J. (1996). Synchronicity: The inner path of leadership. San Francisco, CA: Berrett-Koehler Publishers.

John XXIII (2003, March 16) Angelus message.

John Paul II (1963, April 11). Pacem in terris.

Joseph, E. E. (2006). An exploration of the relationship between servant leadership attributes and leaders' negotiation strategy. Unpublished doctoral dissertation, Regent University, Virginia Beach, VA.

Kanter,R. M. (2008, January). Transforming giants. Harvard Business Review. Leadership Strategy for the Twenty-First Century.

Kiel, D. (2011, January). It takes a hurricane: Might Katrina deliver for New Orleans students what Brown once promised? Journal of Law & Education. Baltimore, MD: Jefferson Law Book Company.

Kipling, R. If. http://www.poetryfoundation.org/poem/175772

Kelly, G. (2008, January-March). Dietrich Bonhoeffer's compassion for the poor. The Living Pulpit.

Kessler, R. (2002, September). Nurturing deep connections; five principles for welcoming soul into school leadership. School Administrator, Vol. 59, No. 8.

Kloehn, S. (1996, November 16). A modern cardinal: Conciliatory skills admired but not always effective. Chicago Tribune [On-line].

Kouzes and Posner (1987). The leadership challenge, First Edition. San Francisco, CA: Jossey-Bass Publishers.

Kouzes and Posner (1995). The leadership challenge, Second Edition. San Francisco, CA: Jossey-Bass Publishers.

Krzyzewski, M. & Phillips, D.T. (2000). Leading with the heart: Coach K's successful strategies for basketball, business, and life. New York: Warner Books.

Kumuyi, W.F. (2007, December). The functions of a servant leader. New African. IC Publications Ltd.

Lafley, A.G. and Charan, R. (2008). The Game-Changer: How You Can Drive Revenue and Profit Growth with Innovation. New York, NY: Crown Business.

Lambert, L. (1995). The constructivist leader. Teachers College Press

Law, W. (2005). Selections from A serious call to a devout and holy life. San Francisco, CA: Harper Collins Publishers.

Lebow, R. (1990). A journey into the heroic environment. Roseville, CA: Prima Publications.

Lenzioni, P. (2002). The five dysfunctions of a team. San Francisco, CA: Jossey-Bass Publishers.

Levinson, D. J. (1986). A conception of adult development. American Psychologist, 41, (1), 3-13.

Lewis, R., Spears, L.C., & Lafferty, B.A. (2008). Myers-Briggs and servant-leadership: The servant-leader and personality type. The Spears Center for Servant Leadership USA and Ralph Lewis Associates.

Lichtenwalner, B. (2022) http://modernservantleader.com/ Ben Lichtenwalner & Radiant Forest, LLC.

Life Application Study Bible (1995). Wheaton, ILL: Tyndale House Publishers, Inc.

Lowe, J. (1996, September). Trust: The invaluable asset. Dallas Business Review, 46-49.

Lundin, S.C. (2001). Fish: A remarkable way to boost morale and improve results. New York. NY: Hyperion Books.

Macciavelli, N. (2003). The Prince. London, UK: Penguin Classics.

MacDonald W. (1995). Believer's bible commentary. Nashville, TN: Thomas Nelson Publishers, Inc.

Macdonald, S. (1996, December 20). Jimmy Carter's heart prefers matters of humanity. The Seattle Times, [On-line}.

Mandela, N. (1999). Long walk to freedom: The Autobiography of Nelson Mandela. New York, NY: Back Bay Books.

Maxwell, J.C. (1999). Becoming a person of influence: How to positively impact the lives of others. United Kingdom: Thomas Nelson & Sons Limited.

Maxwell, J. C. (2002). The Maxwell leadership bible. Nashville, TN: Thomas Nelson, Inc.

Maxwell, J. C. (2010). Everyone communicates, few connect. Nashville, TN: Thomas Nelson, Inc.

McGregor, D. (1960). The human side of enterprise. New York: McGraw Hill.

Mealiea, L. & Baltazar, R. (2005). A strategic guide for building effective teams. Public Personnel Management, 34, (2).

Melrose, K. (1996, April). Leader as servant. Executive Excellence, 13, (4) 20.

Microsoft Competencies (2006). http://www.microsoft.com/education/en-us/training/competencies/pages/default.aspx

Montgomery, J.M. (1992) Life's a Dance. Warner/Reprise Country.

Moseley, D. (2009). Healing relationships: A preaching model. Atlanta, GA: Chalice Press

Nouwen, H. (1989). In the name of Jesus: Reflections on Christian leadership. New York, NY: Crossroad Publishing.

O'Brien, W.J. (2008). Character at work: Building prosperity through the practice of virtue. Mahwah, NJ: Paulist Press.

Palmer, P. J. (2000). Let your life speak. San Francisco, CA: Jossey-Bass Publishers.

Parnell, W. (2019). You may have never worn blackface, but you can still be racist. https://serviceneversleeps.org/about/ Alexandria, VA

Paul, M., & Stroh, D. P. (2007) Managing your time as a leader. [On-line}. Reflections, Volume 7, Number 4. Available: reflections.solonline.org

Peck, M. (1978). The road less traveled. New York, NY: Simon & Shuster, Inc.

Pelicer, L. O., & Anderson, L. W. (1995). A handbook for teacher leaders. Thousand Oaks, CA: Corwin Press, Inc.

Phillips, R. D. (1999). The heart of an executive: Lessons on leadership from the life of King David. New York, NY: Doubleday and Co.

Plessy v. Ferguson (1896). Washington, D.C.: National Archives.

Popescu, D. (2012) Political Action in Václav Havel's thought: The responsibility of resistance. Lanham, MD: Lexington Books.

Raiten-D'Antonio, T. (2004). The velveteen principles: A guide to becoming real. Deerfield Beach, FL: Health Communications, Inc.

Ray, P.H. (1997, February). The emerging culture. American Demographics, [On-line], Available: www.demographics.com/publications/AD/97_AD/9702

Reines, S.H., (2009, January-March). People of many places, sharing one home. The Living Pulpit. New York, NY.

Rigsby, R. (2006). Lessons from a third grade dropout. Nashville, TN: Thomas Nelson.

Robbins, S. P., & Judge, T. A. (2007). Organizational behavior, 12th Edition, Boston, MA: Prentice Hall.

Robinson, W. P. (2002). Leading from the middle. Provo. UT: Executive Excellence Publishing.

Rogers, F. (2003). The world according to Mister Rogers: Important things to remember. New York, NY: Family Communications Inc.

Rogers, J. L. (1992, June). Leadership development for the 90's: Incorporating emergent paradigm perspectives. NASPA Journal, 29, (4), 243-252.

Rost, J. C. (1991). Leadership for the twenty-first century. New York: Praeger Publishers.

Samuel, D. (2008, August 14). Mahatma Gandhi and Christianity. New Delhi, Delhi: Christian Today India.

Sanders, T. (2002). Love is the killer app. New York, NY: Crown Publishing Group.

San Juan, K. S., SJ. (2005) Re-imagining power in leadership: Reflection, integration, and servant leadership. The international journal of servant leadership, Volume 1, Number 1, pp. 187-209. Spokane, WA: Gonzaga University.

Schein, E. H. (2004). Organizational culture and leadership. San Francisco, CA: Jossey-Bass Publishers.

Schein, E. H. (2010). Organizational culture and leadership. San Francisco, CA: Jossey-Bass Publishers.

Schneider, W. (1999, May). Why good management ideas fail-Understanding your corporate culture. Questa, NM: Paradigm Shift International.

Schwahn, C. J., & Spady, W. G. (1998). Total leaders: Applying the best future-focused change strategies to education. Arlington, VA: American Association of School Administrators.

Schwahn, C. J., & Spady, W. G. (2002). Total leaders. Lanham, MD: Scarecrow Press, Inc.

Scripko, R. B. (1992). A moral agent: Bishop as Leader. Unpublished doctoral dissertation, Gonzaga University, Spokane, WA.

Seabrook, K. (2003). Furry logic: A guide to life's little challenges. New York, NY: Ten Speed Press.

Seitz, S. & Pepitone, S. (1996, June). Servant leadership: A model for developing college students. Metropolitan Universities, 6, (4), 113-122.

Senge, P. M. (1990). The fifth discipline: The art and practice of the learning organization. New York: Doubleday.

Senn, L. E., & Childress, J. R. (1999). The secrets of a winning culture. Canada: Leadership Press.

Sergiovanni, T. J. (1992) Moral leadership. San Francisco, CA: Jossey-Bass Publishers.

Sergiovanni, T. J. (1993, January). Frames of leadership. International journal of educational reform, Volume 2, Number 1.

Sire, J. W. (2001). Vaclav Havel: The intellectual conscience of international politics: An introduction, appreciation & critique. Downers Grove, IL: Intervarsity Press.

Sirota, D. (2001). Observations on Mayor Guiliani's leadership in the wake of 9/11. http://www.sirota.com/pdfs/Observations_on_Mayor_Guiliani's_Leadership_in_the_Wake_of_9_11.pdf

Smith, B. (1964). Men of peace. New York: NY: J. B. Lippincott Company.

Synder, D. & Horton, K. (2009). Tom Landry: Man of Character. Grand Island, NE: Cross Training Publishing.

Souba, W. W. (2011). The being of leadership. Philosophy, ethics, and humanities in medicine. http://www.peh-med.com/content/6/1/5.

Spears, L. C. (1995). Reflections on leadership. New York: John Wiley & Sons, Inc.

Spitzer, R. (2000). The spirit of leadership: optimizing creativity and change in organizations. Provo, UT: Executive Excellence Publishing.

Spolsky, J. (2008, December). My style of leadership. Inc. Magazine. Mansueto Ventures LLC.

Starratt, R. (2004). Ethical leadership. San Francisco, CA: John Wiley and Sons.

Stein, G. (2009). The art of racing in the rain. New York, NY: HarperCollins.

Stone, W. C. Differences make a big difference. https://quotefancy.com/william-clement-stone-quotes

Sype, J.W. & Frick, D.M. (2009). Seven pillars of servant leadership: practicing the wisdom of leading by serving. New York, NY: Paulist Press.

Tarr, D. L. (1995). The strategic toughness of servant-leadership. In Spears, Larry C., Reflections on leadership (pp. 79-83). New York: John Wiley & Sons, Inc.

Taylor-Gillham, D. (1998, May). Images of servant leadership in education. Unpublished doctoral dissertation, Northern Arizona University, Flagstaff, AZ.

Tichy, N. M. & Bennis, W. G. (2008). Judgement, how winning leaders make great calls. Penguin Group.

The Priest 2/2011 http://prieststuff.blogspot.com/2011/02/

Tuckman, B. Developmental stages. Bruce Tuckman's Model for Nurturing a Team to High Performance https://www.mindtools.com/pages/article/newLDR_86.htm

Turner, D. (2004, February, 07). Maxims sometimes easiest way to reach heart of the matter. The Seattle Times.

Tutu, D. (2000). Graduation commencement speech at Brandeis University.

Vallotton, K. & Johnson, B. (2006). The supernatural ways of royalty. Shippenburg, PA: Destiny Image Publishers.

Walker, P.D. (1997, April). A case study of servant leadership. Unpublished doctoral dissertation, University of San Francisco. San Francisco, CA.

Wallace, L., & Trinka, J. (2008). A legacy of 21st century leadership. Lincoln, NE: Signature Resources Inc.

Wallis, J. (2004). Baccalaureate: The real struggle is hope vs. cynicism Stanford University, Palo Alto, CA.

Wheatley, M.J. (1994). Leadership and the new science. San Francisco, CA: Berrett-Koehler Publishers.

Wheaton, C.E. (1999). Servant leadership and the public school superintendent. Unpublished doctoral dissertation, Gonzaga University, Spokane, WA.

Wheaton, C.E. (2009). At your service: lessons in leadership. Pittsburg, PA: Dorrance Publishing.

White & Prywes (2007). The nature of leadership; reptiles, mammals, and the challenge of becoming a great leader. New York, NY: Amacom (American Management Association).

Wilkes, C.G. (1998). Jesus on leadership. (Forward by Calvin Miller). Tyndale House Publishing.

Williams, M. (1975). Velveteen rabbit. New York, NY: Doubleday and Co., Inc.

Wing, L. S. (2005). Leadership in high-performance teams. Team performance management, Volume II, No. 1/2.

Womble, S. N. (2005, October/November). Leaving a leadership legacy in Reading Today, Council and affiliate news.

Wooden, J. (2009). Coach Wooden's pyramid to success: Building blocks for a better life. Ventura, CA: Regal Books.

Wright, S. H. (2007, April). Reconciled with atonement. The living pulpit,

Youngs, H. (2007, April). There and back again; my unexpected journey into servant and distributed leadership. Journal of Educational Administration and History Volume 39, No. 1.

Yukl, G. A. (2005). Leadership in organizations. Upper Saddle River, NJ: Pearson-Prentice Hall.

Zander, R. & Zander, B. (2000) The art of possibility. London, England: Penguin Books.

Zinn, H. (2001) History is a weapon: A people's history of the United States. New York, NY: HarperCollins.

Charles E. Wheaton, Ph.D.
School Administrator-Retired
Ph.D. in Educational Leadership, (Servant Leadership)
Gonzaga University, Spokane, WA 5/8/2000
M Ed., Curriculum and Supervision,
1977, Central Washington
University, Ellensburg, WA
B.A.Ed., 1973, Central Washington
University, Ellensburg, WA